ISBN: 978-0-692-61891-2
Publisher: Tradewinds Press
Cover Design: The Chad Barr Group

Confident Giving

—— VOLUME I ——

• • •

Sage Advice for Funders
from One of Philanthropy's Top Advisors

KRIS PUTNAM-WALKERLY, MSW

Praise for *Confident Giving*

We live in a time of massive and accelerating change and no organization or sector is immune to these forces of change. Philanthropy, at its peril, may think it is not affected, and Kris provides hard-earned and deeply thought-through insights that challenge the embedded assumptions and orthodoxies of the field of philanthropy – arriving, in the end at a commonsensical and gentle critique of our field. To gain these insights, a front-to back read is not required, rather, the format allows easy access to any topic that may be top of mind.

— Terry Mazany, President and CEO, Chicago Community Trust

I've known Kris for more than a decade, and have found her thoughts on the field to benefit not just me, but my staff as well. Her insights help us keep our heads focused on our vision and our feet firmly rooted in the communities we serve.

— Bob Eckardt, Executive Vice President, Cleveland Foundation

Kris is skillful in unlocking philanthropy's complexities. Her thoughtful, practical advice provides a roadmap for practitioners who want to increase their effectiveness.

— LaTida Smith, CEO, Moses Taylor Foundation

Kris "gets" philanthropy in a way that few consultants can match. I find her voice and her ideas refreshing, inspiring and always a bright spot of common sense and sanity in a sometimes crazy field.

— Shawn Dove, CEO, Campaign for Black Male Achievement

I have really enjoyed working with Kris over the years, and this book is a perfect encapsulation of much of the wisdom she has shared with our team. It's a go-to on my bookshelf, for sure!

— Susanna Krey, President, Sisters of Charity Foundation of Cleveland

Kris is knowledgeable about all the different, nuanced aspects of philanthropic strategy and understands why not all grantmakers are the same. I appreciate the way she repeatedly brings a fresh perspective to our work.

— Kathy Smith, Senior Program Officer, Walton Family Foundation

Not only have I benefited from Kris' experience and knowledge by reading her postings, but Kris has served on the Community Foundation of Lorain County Board of Directors for the past seven years. Her insights are thought provoking and very practical.

— Brian Frederick, President and CEO, Community Foundation of Lorain County

What I love about Kris's work is that she relates it to common experience, and identifies patterns, themes and strategies in a way that makes you say "ah ha!" No matter how you approach philanthropy, Kris has valuable wisdom to share.

— Lori Kuhn, Executive Director, Morgan Family Foundation

In *Confident Giving* Kris offers direct and straightforward advice to improve foundation practices. Her perspective and insights on a breadth of topics, from strategy and leadership to evaluation and grant processes, are valuable for both new and experienced trustees, CEOs, and staff.
— **Christy Pichel, former CEO, Stuart Foundation**

Kris's thoughts on our field are refreshing, provocative, and compelling. This collection will make you think in new and welcome ways.
— **Alison Belfrage, Executive Director, Ohio State Bar Foundation**

Kris brings the perfect combination of bold visioning ability and attention to detail to her writing, which is why we've used her work (and her services) to develop a clearer, more engaging strategy for growing our organization's reach and impact.
— **Deborah Ellwood, President and CEO, CFLeads**

In a field where "smart" often translates to "unreadable," Kris's writing is down-to-earth and to-the-point, sharing pearls of wisdom you'll actually enjoy reading.
— **Merle Gordon, Director of Community Programs & Public Affairs, HealthSpan**

I find the wisdom in Kris's newsletter to be inspiring—so much so that I hired her firm to help our foundation tell our own inspiring story. The fresh perspective that Kris brings to philanthropy is always eye-opening and spot-on.
— **Allen Smart, Vice President of Programs, Kate B. Reynolds Charitable Trust**

On many occasions, the *Confident Giving* newsletters have been timely, current, and precisely what I needed to inform our foundation's philanthropic strategy. The pieces on communications, grantmaking evaluation, and strategy formation have been at once insightful and entertaining.
— **Rhonnel Sotelo, Executive Director, Rogers Family Foundation**

As grantmakers, we often get tunnel vision. Kris shines that proverbial light at the end of the tunnel, calling us to be more honest, effective, and fulfilled in our philanthropy.
— **Sherece West-Scantlebury, President and CEO, Winthrop Rockefeller Foundation**

Having known and worked with Kris for years, I'm always eager to find *Confident Giving* in my inbox. The ideas she shares are easy to read and engaging to think about—and have shown me many ways to improve our own strategies.
— **Nonet Sykes, Director of Race, Equity, and Inclusion, Annie E. Casey Foundation**

Table of Contents

• • •

Introduction

In my line of work, I am fortunate enough to witness firsthand the soaring triumphs and epic failures that accompany any undertaking as potentially uncertain as giving away philanthropic dollars. I'm also surprised by the number of people who want to "do philanthropy" the right way—but who hesitate (or simply don't think) to invest the time and money to learn about what works best for others and might make their own work more effective and deliver greater impact.

To help fill that void, and to make the practical lessons of effective philanthropy more readily accessible to busy grantmakers, I started the *Confident Giving*® weekly e-newsletter at the beginning of 2014. About 18 months and closing in on 100 editions later, the readership of *Confident Giving* has grown by leaps and bounds, and hardly a week goes by that someone in the philanthropic community doesn't reach out to comment on its content.

Grantmaking is a complex and complicated undertaking, and my goal is to help make it as simple and effective as possible— with an eye always on the prize of delivering the greatest impact possible for the communities my clients serve. With that in mind, I've collected the best of the *Confident Giving* newsletter content from its first 18 months and compiled it into this book.

Of course, I can't pretend that all of the ideas within these pages originated solely within my own brain. I've had the benefit of many wise counselors, colleagues, and mentors who have contributed greatly to the process. In particular, I am indebted to Alan Weiss, for helping me live a life of abundance; Steven Gaffney, for telling me to let it out; Val Wright, for encouraging me to be ruthless; Phil Symcych, for providing an example; Henry A.J. Ramos, for starting me on my consulting career; Alexa Cortez Culwell, for being my first client; Caroline Krauskopf, for seeing my possibilities before I did; my parents, Ginny Putnam and Dean Putnam, for raising me to believe I could do anything I wanted; and especially my husband Terry Walkerly, for his nonstop love, encouragement, and support. This book would not be possible without the extraordinary writing talent of Elizabeth Russell; expert copyediting assistance of Mary VanClay; and the Chad Barr Group's strategic and transformative design of my website, newsletter, and this book.

It is my hope that by sharing this collected, collective wisdom, both institutional and individual grantmakers might recognize a certain theme or idea that will spark an "ah-ha!" moment that helps them confidently propel their giving forward.

Leadership

DO YOU HAVE A POVERTY MENTALITY OR AN ABUNDANCE MENTALITY?

I've spoken with thousands of foundation leaders over the past 15 years, and I've found that one thing holds many back from achieving the dramatic success and deep impact that they seek. They have a poverty mentality rather than an abundance mentality.

In a nutshell, a poverty mentality stems from a misguided belief that maintaining a Spartan operation equates to delivering value for grantees and communities. An abundance mentality is a belief that internal investment is important, and the more you put into your operation, the more you get out of it.

I don't believe the poverty or abundance mentalities really have much to do with money. Instead, they have everything to do with attitude and outlook. Consider these examples:

Foundation leaders with a poverty mentality will say things like:

- We're just a small organization; we can't afford it (even on something of strategic importance to the organization).
- The money we spend on professional development or technology is money we're taking away from our grantees (even if investing in yourself would make you a smarter, more effective grantmaker better able to achieve your mission).
- Our grantee budgets cannot include more than 12 percent for administrative overhead (regardless of the project and what they are trying to accomplish).
- We don't provide our staff with laptops when they travel for business—what if they break? (It doesn't matter that customer service suffers when grant proposals stack up and emails go unanswered because employees can't efficiently make use of their travel time.)
- What is the cheapest way we can do this (regardless of quality, time, or discomfort)?

Grantmakers with an abundance mentality will say things like:

- Who are the top experts in the country (or world) who can advise us?
- How much more impact could we have if we added additional staffing capacity to our grantmaking initiative? Who are the best people we can get, and what is the most strategic use of their time?
- If our program were to become a national model, what would that look like? What can we put in place now to accomplish that?

- If we really want to make a difference on this issue, we need to make a multi-year commitment.
- What tools, resources, or technology will help our staff and grantees become more effective?
- Let's magnify our impact by leveraging relationships and partners.
- Let's survey our grantees to better understand their experience with us, so that we can improve.
- It's OK if this corporate funding initiative also benefits our competitors. It will improve outcomes for everyone and we will learn a lot.

Reflect for a minute on the personalities and accomplishments of the organizations and leaders you know that operate with a poverty mentality, then think about those who embrace an abundance mentality. Which one would you rather lead or be part of? Me, too!

●   ●   ●

DELUSIONAL ALTRUISM

Foundations pride themselves on the good they do for others; that's the very nature and culture of philanthropy. However, in my 16 years of experience advising foundations, I've found that most foundations suffer from delusional altruism.

Delusional altruism is when you are genuinely trying to help people—but paying absolutely no attention to the operational inefficiency and waste that drains grantseekers or your own foundation of the human and financial capital necessary to accomplish these goals. **Let me give you three examples:**

1. A foundation gave itself five weeks to approve a Request for Proposals (RFP) that it had already written, but it gave grantseekers only three weeks to apply. Five different departments within a large national foundation each had a week to modify—or simply

sign off on—an RFP. By contrast, each applicant had to decide whether to apply, decide whether to do so jointly with other invited applicants, develop the proposal concept (possibly in collaboration), write the proposal, and get written commitments of matching funding—all within three weeks.

2. A foundation evaluation director sent an RFP to 50 evaluators to conduct a $40,000 evaluation. The evaluation director had pre-qualified a "mere" 50 evaluators and therefore received an overwhelming volume of proposals that he had to sort through and vet. Then he had to determine finalists and interview them, all before he could make a decision and actually hire someone. This left him exhausted, overwhelmed, and behind on other projects. It probably took him six months, whereas the evaluation itself could have been done in that time. He and his associate likely spent half of the $40,000 project fee just on their own staff time.

3. A foundation pays a program officer $60 per hour to perform tasks that an administrative assistant could handle for $20 per hour. Countless foundations pride themselves on their low overhead and administrative costs. They insist that one program assistant can support two to four senior leaders who each are responsible for allocating millions of dollars in funding annually. What this really means is that program executives spend their time scheduling meetings, proofreading documents, collating binders, updating PowerPoint decks, taking notes, and filling out travel reimbursement forms. This is time not spent developing new relationships, identifying ways to leverage funding, sourcing new ideas, mitigating risk, thinking, and planning. If the administrative activities could be done for $40 per hour less, the foundation is essentially robbing itself of this money—and exhausting its staff along the way.

In none of these cases was the foundation paying any attention to the drain on human and financial capital in operations and the execution of their grantmaking efforts.

Do you suffer from altruistic delusion? Here are three easy ways to find out:

1. Ask yourself. Take a project you feel is truly worthwhile. Spend an hour thinking about all the people, paper, committees, handoffs, sign-offs, write-ups, etc., that are involved. Identify three ways to simplify the process.

2. Ask your staff. Ask your staff to do the same thing, on their own or in a staff meeting. Allow these to be big ideas as well as small solutions, and allow for anonymous idea submissions. Prioritize a few ideas, act on them, then discuss with staff what impact the changes had.

3. Ask your grantees. Ask grantees to identify times when they felt the foundation wasn't being realistic, or when the process seemed unfair. Ask them to help you identify solutions, too. They'll want to answer anonymously; use grantseeker surveys or interviews conducted by a third-party consultant.

I guarantee that if you can suspend your belief in your own pure altruism and examine ways you might be deluding yourself, you will be delighted with the dramatic improvements your foundation can make on the issues and communities you so clearly care about.

● ● ●

ONE MISTAKE FAMILY FOUNDATIONS SHOULD AVOID

A new, large family foundation is about to hire its first executive. The foundation board thinks "any manager," such as an attorney, a bank executive, or a business consultant, would be perfectly qualified for the job—no philanthropy experience necessary. Sound familiar? Too often smart and talented people are extraordinarily successful in business, and then fail to apply their smarts to their philanthropic giving. **I advised them to ask the following three questions:**

1. What is the business that allowed the donor to create so much wealth that he or she could start a foundation? Whatever it is, how successful would it have been if they had handed the role of CEO over to just "any manager" with no experience in that industry? If they can't imagine doing that for their business, then they shouldn't consider doing it for the foundation.

2. How much time and money do they want to spend on "any manager" as he or she moves up the steep learning curve about philanthropy and operating a foundation? Wouldn't they rather hit the ground running?

3. Are they willing to risk the foundation's reputation on someone who has no experience doing this job? Often the foundation's name is the same as the donor's name. "Any manager" could fumble a lot before getting it right.

In any industry, it's great to bring in fresh ideas, perspectives, and talent. And philanthropy has a lot to learn from other sectors on topics such as customer service, innovation, and technology. But don't disrespect the power and promise of philanthropy by hiring unqualified people to lead it.

● ● ●

ARE YOU A NEW PHILANTHROPY CEO? DON'T MAKE THESE FIVE MISTAKES

I've worked with many new foundation CEOs, some of whom are not only new to their role, but new to philanthropy. If you find yourself in this position, here are five mistakes you should avoid:

1. **Assuming you don't need to learn about philanthropy because you were hired for being "an outsider."** There is a trend in philanthropy to pooh-pooh philanthropy: a belief that philanthropy is too insular, which isn't entirely untrue. Every field needs to bring in fresh thinking and new ideas, and one way to accomplish that is to hire from outside. But that doesn't mean that the field is damaged. Giving money away is not easy. Recognize that you are standing on the shoulders of seasoned leaders with vast experience in grantmaking. Find the strengths in your foundation, your team, your funding collaborative, and your grantmaking strategies so that you know what to preserve and what to change. There is much to be learned from the experiences, best practices, and mistakes of others.

2. **Not reaching out to colleagues.** A few years ago I had lunch with a foundation CEO client and discussed my new project with another foundation in the same city whose CEO had recently been hired from the nonprofit sector. "Funny," my client said. "This is his first philanthropy job. He's been there four months, but he

hasn't reached out to me even though our foundations are working on similar issues. In fact, I've heard the same concern from other funders. They are a major player in this community—why wouldn't he introduce himself to the other big foundations?" If you are new to the field, identify the top ten foundations in your community, the top ten in your program areas (e.g., if you fund regionally or internationally), and other key funding partners. Make a point to contact those CEOs, take them to lunch, schedule a phone conversation, or set a time to talk at a meeting you both will be attending. These colleagues can be invaluable resources to you to help orient you to your new role and to philanthropy. They might be willing to provide insight into your foundation, identify opportunities, introduce you to other colleagues, and partner with you. You have nothing to lose and everything to gain.

3. **Insulting your colleagues.** One new CEO, during a conference call with seasoned foundation leaders in his community, made a comment that philanthropy needs to change to finally have some impact. One of these foundations has been making grants for more than 100 years, and the other for more than 60. Their CEOs have been in their jobs for well over a decade each. I'm guessing that they each have achieved some impact! While there is always room for improvement, running out the gate by insulting your colleagues is not the best way to start. Instead, take the time to research your colleague foundations' strengths and accomplishments and identify ways that, collectively, you can all make improvements.

4. **Not recognizing that you have entered a new industry full of connections and networks.** You don't know what you don't know. So recognize that and act accordingly. A consultant colleague was introduced to a new CEO by his vice president, and after a wonderful

conversation they agreed the consultant should submit a proposal to help with a project of strategic importance to the foundation. She submitted it, and waited for a response. And waited. Despite multiple phone calls, voice messages, and emails over a period of two months, she never heard from him. What this person failed to appreciate is that she was highly connected and well respected in that community and personally knew several of his staff, some board members, and many of his colleagues. Treating her poorly reflected badly on him. He walked into a new field without appreciating the existing networks and interconnectivity within it. He didn't have to hire her, but rather than leveraging existing networks, he ignored them.

5. **Refusing help.** Taking a new position is risky, and I am sure you are eager to prove yourself. There are a tremendous number of resources that can help you, if you are willing to put your ego aside and accept help. This could involve executive coaching, seeking advice from colleagues, finding more seasoned philanthropy CEOs who can serve as mentors, hiring consultants to support your initial goals (e.g., to review the impact of current funding strategies or help with planning), or taking advantage of the many learning opportunities in the field. For example, look into the following resources that best meet your particular needs:

- LearnPhilanthropy provides a wealth of free resources to accelerate learning among newcomers to philanthropy.
- The Council on Foundations offers resources for CEO leadership development and foundation management.
- If you are running a family foundation, the National Center on Family Philanthropy offers the CEO Initiative.

- CEOs of small foundations can participate in Exponent Philanthropy's Master Juggler Executive Institute.
- The National Network of Consultants to Grantmakers provides a free online directory of philanthropy consultants and advisors.
- New leaders who are under age 40 might consider joining Emerging Practitioners in Philanthropy.
- If you are running a community foundation, you can attend the Community Foundation Fundamentals course sponsored by the Council on Foundations.
- Your local regional association of grantmakers might offer programming and support specifically for foundation CEOs or those new to philanthropy. For example, Northern California Grantmakers offers the New Grantmakers Institute.

The bottom line: You bring new strengths to your foundation and to a field that has a history of significant impact. And you also have room to learn, grow, and improve, just as your foundation and the entire philanthropic sector have opportunities to strengthen and improve. If you take the time to learn about your new world, and your role in it, you will be positioned for tremendous success.

● ● ●

EIGHT QUESTIONS TO IMPROVE YOUR PHILANTHROPIC GIVING THIS YEAR

Every new year, I speak with many philanthropic leaders about their goals and hopes for the coming year. By the end of January, those goals and hopes have become a blur for many. Some entered the New Year running and are starting to feel overwhelmed. A few are experiencing a sluggish start. Others aren't sure where to begin. That's completely understandable—philanthropy is hard work! However, taking a little time for planning can help you achieve dramatic results this year.

The next time January rolls around, ask yourself these eight questions:

1. **What can I learn in the next three months?** These should be things that will improve your grantmaking for the remainder of the year. You might need to conduct an evaluation, retain an expert advisor, or spend the day reading articles and listening to podcasts about a certain topic. Armed with new insight, you will be better prepared to allocate your talent, time, and resources and achieve more dramatic results.

2. **What holds me back?** Identify and eliminate it. If you are overwhelmed by email, commit to reaching "Inbox Zero" by the end of January. Do you have a poverty mentality, believing you don't deserve or can't afford something that would greatly improve your work experience? Are you hesitant to seek a promotion because you fear you don't have the leadership skills? Hire an executive coach, talk to a therapist, take a class—do whatever it takes to move past this self-created hurdle so that you can be happier and accomplish more.

3. **How can I empower my staff?** From the vice president of programs to the administrative assistant, your staff could have greater impact if they felt they had the authority and the training to do so. This could involve increasing program staff's budget and grantmaking authority, eliminating bureaucratic hurdles within your operation, training assistants in customer service and allowing them to resolve problems, or rethinking your entire HR function to strategically develop leadership at all levels of your foundation. The changes can be big or small, and the best source of ideas is your staff.

4. **What can I share?** You've benefited from the wisdom and knowledge of experts, nonprofit leaders, and

community members who helped you shape your grantmaking strategy. Now it's time to pay it forward by sharing what you've learned with colleagues who can benefit from your insight. Write a case study or create a funder toolkit to share what your foundation has accomplished, what you've learned, and what you would do differently.

5. **If I could only accomplish one thing this year, what would it be?** That really gets to the heart of it, doesn't it? You might be at your organization for the next ten years, but what if this were your last year? What do you really want to accomplish? For what do you wish to be remembered? Write it down, schedule time in your calendar, retain the help you need, and go do it.

6. **What are my top three priorities for the year?** (If you find it hard to pick only three, refer to the previous item!). I'm not saying you can't work on the other four, seven, or ten things. But now that you know your top priorities, you can determine what steps you can take in Q1 to make sure they happen by Q4. For example, if you want to launch a new grantmaking initiative, you might need to retain a consultant to conduct an environmental scan. If you want to change, expand, or eliminate a funding strategy, you might want to evaluate it first to assess impact and opportunity. At the very least, create a time line starting with what you want to accomplish by year's end and work backward.

7. **What is the one thing I can do now that will make everything else easier or unnecessary?** In my experience, this often involves delegation: taking the time to hire or train someone today who can begin taking work off your plate. But it could also mean firing someone, reorganizing your team, recruiting new board members, investing in coaching or leadership development, et

8. **What activity consistently takes an obnoxious amount of time and drains energy from me and my team?** You know what I'm talking about. It's that activity that just popped into your head. That thing that you dread doing every year, quarter, or month. Identify three ways you can reduce its intensity or eliminate it entirely. Is your board book 200 pages long? Develop a plan to reduce it to 50. Are your proposals cumbersome to read? Streamline them. Yes, this will take time, but if you start that project now, by the end of the year your staff will consider you their hero. More important, you will free up time and mental energy to accomplish your top priorities.

I guarantee that if you answer and act upon these eight questions- preferably within the first quarter - you will reap the rewards during the remainder of the year.

I'VE FOUND ONE THING HOLDS MANY FOUNDATION LEADERS BACK FROM ACHIEVING THE DRAMATIC SUCCESS AND DEEP IMPACT THAT THEY SEEK. THEY HAVE A POVERTY MENTALITY RATHER THAN AN ABUNDANCE MENTALITY.

Strategy

CLARITY TRUMPS STRATEGY

I'm a highly organized person and can spend endless hours creating strategies, with corresponding tactics, time lines, and to-do lists. But in my experience, one thing trumps strategy: clarity. You can have all the strategies, logic models, and theories of change in the world, but you won't get far if you aren't crystal clear inside your head about what you are trying to accomplish.

Let me give you two quick examples from my life, neither of which has anything to do with philanthropy.

Many years ago I was in an unhealthy relationship. For five years. Thousands of dollars of therapy later, it wasn't until I had clarity that this person wasn't going to change, that I needed to get out, and that I deserved a better life that I had the courage to end it. The days, weeks, and months that followed were painful, but it didn't matter. I was clear I was doing the right thing. That clarity kept me calm and focused, and it guided all of my decisions. I never looked back.

Fast forward eight years, and I decided to relocate my life and business from the San Francisco Bay Area to Cleveland, Ohio, where I was going to get engaged, become a stepmom, and live in a new city where I had no friends and few business relationships. I had to sell my house, say good-bye to all my friends, and communicate this move to my clients without losing their business. All in a span of three months, during which I maintained a full consulting practice. I recall it as being one of the most stressful times of my life, and I had to wake up at 3:00 a.m. almost every day to get it all done. What got me through it? Total clarity that I was doing the right thing for me. My friends questioned my sanity, and my business coach suggested I give myself more time. But I was clear on what I wanted in my life (marry my now-husband and be closer to my family), so all of my decisions were easy, my strategies were obvious, and I stayed focused on my goal.

Once you have clarity, the strategies and tactics will follow fairly quickly. Without clarity, you can be all over the map. If you know that you want to help high school students successfully graduate high school and enter the workforce, your strategies might include increasing graduation rates (reducing absenteeism, supporting academic credit recovery), career exposure and experience (job training, job shadowing, internships, summer jobs), and helping students get into college (college visits, application support, SAT and

ACT tutoring). But if you can't decide whether you want to help kids get jobs, reduce teenage pregnancy, reduce youth violence, or provide universal pre-K to all four-year-olds, you won't get very far.

All are important and will help young people successfully graduate and transition into adulthood.

But if you aren't clear, you are stuck and you can't help anyone.

How do you get clarity? Well, that's a tough one. Just like "lucky" people are actually people who put themselves in situations where they can easily take advantage of new opportunities (they constantly learn, network, are open to new ideas, etc.), I think clarity comes when we keep ourselves informed, try new things, practice trusting our instincts, are self-aware, and are disciplined in making decisions. You can't force yourself into clarity any more than you can force yourself into falling in love.

Look at some important decisions you need to make in the next few months. Whether it's deciding how to focus your grantmaking initiative or where to send your child to school, ask yourself if you have clarity about your decision. If not, why not? Have you given yourself the time and space to think about it? Sought the advice of trusted colleagues or friends? Armed yourself with enough data to make an informed decision? Given yourself permission to follow your instinct? If you haven't done these things, do them now.

●　　●　　●

WE NEED STRATEGY AND JUDGMENT, NOT TOOLS AND TACTICS

Philanthropy and nonprofit leaders continue jumping on tools and tactics, when strategy and judgment are needed.

Let me give you a few examples of what I mean:

- **Infographics:** I'm all for finding visual and creative ways to educate people, but for the past few years people have jumped on the infographic bandwagon as if it were a solution for all information sharing. As a result, I've seen documents so crammed full of graphics and percentages they make my head spin. Not everything needs an infographic.

- **Crowdfunding:** A foundation program officer told me that her foundation decided they "need to do crowdfunding" and therefore the new initiative she wanted me to help her design "needs to include crowdfunding." Crowdfunding can be a great tool, depending upon what you are trying to accomplish. But this foundation was forcing this tool onto its grantmaking, with no appreciation for whether it was a good fit.

- **Ice Bucket Challenge:** For all its flaws, the Ice Bucket Challenge did raise extraordinary amounts of money and identified new donors for ALS. However, many nonprofit fund-raisers are now expected to come up with similar gimmicks to raise funds and visibility for their causes. For most, the success of ALS will be impossible to replicate. And, more important, nonprofits should focus on strategic fund development and not divert resources to hopping on the latest fund-raising craze.

- **Social media:** I am frequently asked by foundation staff, "Should we be on Twitter?" My answer is always the same: What are you trying to communicate, who is your audience, and is Twitter a good way to reach them? I also ask if they have any communications capacity (staff or consultants) or a communications plan. Twitter—or any form of social media—is a tool. Rather than grabbing at it, it is far better to come up with a comprehensive communications plan (with objectives, strategies, audiences, and tactics) and see where social media fits, or doesn't, in that plan.

- **Collective impact:** A foundation CEO told me that she was looking for an initiative that would be a good fit for a collective impact approach. I like the collective impact model. However, you don't search for social problems to tackle so that you can try out a new model. First determine your goals and strategies, and then figure out the best way to get there. If the collective impact approach will help, that's great. But you don't need to convene stakeholders, fund a backbone organization, and create shared measurement systems if you can tackle the problem by funding several organizations that are already doing great work.

When confronted with the latest philanthropic craze, take the time to understand it and see what it has to offer. But then ask yourself these four questions.

- **Why?**
- **What is our goal?**
- **What is our strategy?**
- **What is the best way to get there?**

If you thoughtfully answer these questions, you will stay focused on your objectives, incorporate new tools and ideas only when they can advance your efforts, and avoid diverting human and financial resources on approaches that take you off track.

SPECIAL OPS: FIVE SITUATIONS FOR DEPLOYING A RED TEAM

We all need friends and colleagues who have our backs. When we're going out on a limb, we need support. But maybe we need something else, too. Maybe we need someone who can think like the enemy.

The CIA calls it the "Red Team." The military, the Federal Aviation Administration, and major corporations like IBM also use the term to refer to a group designed to penetrate your defenses—with your enthusiastic approval. This idea isn't often discussed in philanthropy circles, but I believe it holds tremendous value for us.

In information technology, a Red Team might be the hackers who try to break into a system; in the military, the Red Team plays the role of the enemy trying to overcome your defenses. In any organization, a Red Team is charged with finding out what can go wrong, where the holes are, and why what you're trying to do won't work. The point is to question your assumptions, plans, operations, concepts, and capabilities. The purpose, of course, is to increase the effectiveness of your organization or your project by uncovering why something won't work so that you can either fix it or abandon it, before you become irreparably entangled. This goes beyond the typical due diligence often done by foundations.

Here are five situations in which a funder should have a Red Team:

1. **There's a lot of money on the line.** Perhaps you're making a very large grant, significantly higher than most that you make. Maybe it's one of the largest

grants in your foundation's history. Are you sure you've considered all the holes that money could fall into, or do you need to bring another level head or two to the table before you hand out the cash?

2. **The foundation's reputation is at stake.** Perhaps you are taking on a controversial issue, or maybe you're taking the lead in your community to solve a particular problem. Have you thought through all the implications clearly? Do you need someone who can look at your actions through the eyes of, say, a local news reporter hunting for a juicy story?

3. **A project will use a lot of your foundation's internal resources.** Perhaps it will draw a significant amount of your CEO's time, or it will need involvement from multiple departments, diverting them from other important work. Who has helped you think through what this will mean for staff morale and productivity?

4. **You can't walk away.** Perhaps you're thinking of committing to a five-year project to fund technology upgrades for schools in disadvantaged neighborhoods. You are going to need to stick with it, and not pull the plug midway (e.g., leaving schools with new technology but no training to use it). A Red Team could help you identify unforeseen obstacles that could sabotage the project in early stages, or conclude that this is not the best use of your philanthropic resources.

5. **You're responding to an emergency—or a perceived emergency.** The community you serve has been hard hit by an unexpected storm or other disaster, and suddenly you're tempted to rechannel your support. But you're not an emergency-response unit. Do you have advisors who can help you think through the results of a knee-jerk reaction, no matter how well intended?

A Red Team doesn't have to be complicated. It does need to involve smart people who are given permission to kick the tires—and to do so quickly. What are you working on right now that could use a Red Team? Who are three individuals you could call tomorrow to be on your Red Team? And how might they help you avoid costly mistakes? A Red Team isn't always necessary, but when you need one, its contribution is invaluable.

• • •

HOW TO STRIKE FEAR IN THE HEARTS OF GRANTEES

In my experience, few words strike fear in the hearts of foundation grantees like the following, when dropped from a program officer's lips: We're about to start a strategic planning process.

I can almost hear the screams of terror here in my top-secret vacation retreat spot. And who can blame them?

A funder undergoing strategic planning often pulls the rug out from under grantees, at least temporarily, while the funder "suspends grantmaking" for a few months or even a year to "evaluate priorities and approaches." During that time, grantees might be asked to answer questions about their work, participate in discussion or focus groups, or even (gulp) share their opinions with funders in person. And all the while, the foremost question on a grantee's mind must be, "Will they still continue to fund our organization?"

It's not that strategic planning is a bad idea. In fact, many funders might even benefit from doing it more often (some even for the first time). But strategic planning usually means some kind of change—amplifying efforts in one area, diminishing them in another, realigning the ways in which the foundation interacts with the nonprofit community, changing the funding model to focus more deeply but less broadly. It's understandable that funded nonprofits might get nervous, but there are some things that funders can do to help soothe nerves and alleviate uncertainty. When starting your strategic planning process:

1. **Communicate early and often.** No one likes surprises—at least, not when they have to do with a potential loss of funding. The earlier you can let your grantees know that you are going to engage in a strategic planning process, the more time they have to get used to the idea and prepare. As your process unfolds, it will help mitigate rumors and create buy-in if you continue to provide updates and possibly share the research that will ultimately inform your new plan. If nonprofits and community leaders understand the challenges your research reveals, or the lack of impact a "sacred cow" program delivers, they may be more willing to back your new strategic direction.

2. **Be transparent.** Why are you undergoing planning, and why now? What process will you use, and how long will it take? By answering these questions, you at the very least will give your grantees and indication of how long they might feel uneasy. Answer questions as honestly and directly as you can. If you can't answer a question right away, say so—then get back to the questioner as soon as the time is right.

3. **Be direct.** Are you anticipating major changes in your grantmaking or internal organization? If so, say so. If not, say so. Being honest about what grantees might expect helps them get over their negative reactions faster and embrace the fact that change is coming. You can help by connecting grantees to potential new partners and new sources of support that might benefit them during and after your planning process.

4. Be quick. Taking a year off from grantmaking to evaluate your own impact and strategy is incredibly hard on grantees. The faster you can get to your new plan, the better for everyone. If you feel the need to explore aspects of your work more deeply over a longer period of time, consider doing so while the wheels are still rolling, then use the lessons and observations you're gathering in real time to inform your new strategy.

5. Don't become invisible. Locking yourself away from grantees will hurt your ability to build trust in your new strategic plan. Before you go into planning mode, meet with grantees in person to let them know—or at the very least, pick up the phone. Don't rely on email to shield you from delivering unpleasant or unwelcome news. As your planning process progresses, make sure you're still present in your community and among your grantees. Just because your grantmaking is on hiatus doesn't mean your individual caring and camaraderie should be. There are many ways to support your community personally and professionally beyond day-to-day foundation work. Make new connections between grantees, talk about a community issue over lunch, and yes, answer countless questions about how your strategic planning is going.

The more you prepare grantees for a foundation's strategic planning process and the more you continue to communicate during the process, the better your chances that your plan will be well received and endorsed by your grantee community. Even if you won't make everyone happy with your new direction, you will have at least given them the information and warning they need to develop their own responses.

BRINGING YOUR NEW STRATEGIC PLAN ONLINE WITHOUT ALIENATING YOUR COMMUNITY

I wrote above about the phrase that terrifies grantees: "We're about to start a strategic planning process." Although I listed many things that you can do to help mitigate grantee angst during a strategic planning process, the work doesn't stop when the final plan is approved.

It's likely that many grantees who relied on your funding in the past may not be part of your future plan, or they will constitute a much smaller percentage of your grantmaking budget. If that's the case, don't make hearing the news like ripping off a Band-aid. Instead, make sure your new strategic plan rollout includes short-term strategies to help your grantees navigate the transition. **For example:**

Communicate your new priorities clearly. Before sharing your new strategic plan with anyone outside your foundation, be sure to develop a set of clear, consistent messages that explain the following:

- **Why you've settled on a new direction (you've determined you'll deliver more value for the community by sharpening/broadening your focus).**

- **How you got there (by including input from multiple stakeholders).**

- **When the change in direction will take effect (you'll honor current multi-year commitments).**

- **Who is affected (although you may no longer fund some organizations, they still deliver value and are worthy of support).**

Break the news in person. Yes, looking a former grantee in the eye and explaining why his organization is no longer a fit for your foundation is uncomfortable, but you are both members of the philanthropic community and you own him that courtesy and respect. This is not a job for email. Plus, if you've take the step above and created clear messages, your grantee will understand.

Spend down gradually. There's no rule that says you have to pull the plug all at once. Consider reducing a grantee's allocation incrementally over time as you simultaneously work to increase investments elsewhere. This gives outgoing grantees time to plan and prepare and your new grantees and program staff a chance to grow more intentionally.

Provide bridge grants. When I was consulting to the Charles and Helen Schwab Foundation, we used bridge grants to help grantees transition to new sources of funding. This gave them a way to prepare for change mentally and fiscally and ensured that they did not feel that the rug was pulled out from under them by the shift in focus.

Consider capacity building. If your foundation supported a particular aspect of nonprofit operations, such as leadership development or technology training, consider offering short-term (one-year) grants to help nonprofit staff amp up that capacity internally. Even if you don't have this kind of grant history to build on, consider capacity building support for fund development functions—especially since grantees will need skills to replace the funds they'll no longer receive from you. This has the added bonus of building on your previous investment and turning the nonprofit staff in question from laymen to experts.

Offer general operating support. Although not as targeted as some of the other strategies for easing away from grantees, general operating support is always welcome, and it can allow grantees to adjust as they see fit to this new change in their operating environment. Plus, providing operating support with no strings or expectations attached sends the message that even though their work and your strategy no longer align, you still think they're valuable and you trust their judgment.

Like the old song says, breaking up is hard to do. Ending a professional relationship with a grantee can be just as emotionally trying as ending more personal one. But using the strategies above can help make for a smoother transition for all, and smooth ruffled feathers to boot.

IN MY EXPERIENCE, FEW WORDS STRIKE FEAR IN THE HEARTS OF FOUNDATION GRANTEES LIKE THE FOLLOWING: "WE'RE ABOUT TO START A STRATEGIC PLANNING PROCESS."

Grantmaking

If your to-do list includes "increase the impact of our giving," read on! Below are five grantmaking mistakes you should avoid.

1. **Jumping on the latest philanthropy craze.** Every year a new set of tools and ideas emerge that become the hot trends (think infographics, collective impact, Ice Bucket Challenge, crowdfunding, social media), and grantmakers feel compelled to try them out. A grantmaker told me that her foundation decided they "need to do crowdfunding" and therefore the new initiative she wanted me to help her design "must include crowdfunding," but she wasn't even sure what that meant. Crowdfunding can be a great tool, depending upon what you are trying to accomplish. But this foundation was forcing it onto its grantmaking, with no appreciation for whether it was a good fit.

When confronted with the latest philanthropic craze, take the time to understand it and see what it has to offer. But then ask yourself these four questions. What is our goal? What is our strategy? What is the best way to get there? Will this tool help?

2. **Only giving one grant per nonprofit**, no matter how much impact they have, in order to spread funds to all the nonprofits in your area. That is the belief of one family foundation, which refuses to ever give a second grant to a nonprofit. It's noble to want to help many causes. But at the end of the day, what do your grants amount to? Nothing comes of the grantee-funder relationship that develops, the nonprofit is left in the same position as before your grant, and as the funder you aren't achieving impact in any area.

3. **Leaving your funding partners in the lurch.** It takes sustained effort for funders to develop and maintain successful funding partnerships with each other. Rarely do these involve formal arrangements such as MOUs; it is far more common for the partnerships to be forged on trust and verbal agreements. Breaking that trust can lead to serious ramifications that reach far beyond the activity at hand. One corporate funder of a local collaborative agreed for weeks to jointly pay the costs of a seasoned consultant to quickly plan a critical, time-sensitive event. She balked at the cost ($5,000) and backed out at the last minute, forcing the other foundations to scramble and their nonprofit partner to donate part of their grant to cover the costs. If you decide to partner with other funders, recognize the hard work and strategic maneuvering they have contributed and reward them by being a partner they can depend on. You might not agree with every decision and every dollar, but if you focus on the big picture you can avoid alienating your most important allies.

4. **Giving yourself five months to prepare a Request for Proposals (RFP), but giving the applicants three weeks to apply.** This is a very common mistake, and five months is being generous (it's often 10 or 12). Frequently, the funders' own lack of time management leads to the compressed time line for grantees, putting the squeeze on the very organizations that help funders achieve their missions. If it takes you that long to summarize what you want to accomplish with your funding strategy and outline your funding guidelines, imagine how long it will take nonprofits to respond. You need to make two changes immediately: (1) Reduce your internal bureaucracy and decision-making time, and (2) be kinder to your grantseekers by providing a more realistic time line that allows them to prepare a well-researched and thoughtful response.

5. **Hiring a more expensive consultant simply because she charges more.** I was once told by a program officer, "We decided to go with the more expensive consultant. She thinks this project will take longer to do (more hours), so we think she must know something that you don't." (This despite the fact I had done this project before and knew exactly what was involved, and my lower fee was a fixed price!). Consultants who take longer to accomplish your objectives aren't necessarily better—perhaps they are just slower! Don't confuse expense with expertise.

I can't make this stuff up! Grantmaking isn't easy, but it does require common sense. If you created a policy five years ago that is no longer applicable or hinders your work, change it. If you want to make a difference, develop a grantmaking strategy that rewards impact and accomplishment, not mere existence. And if you want to be part of effective partnerships, then be an effective partner.

DOES YOUR GRANTMAKING INITIATIVE TAKE INITIATIVE?

You're designing a new philanthropic initiative and you expect results quickly. Which adjectives would you rather described your team?

Option 1: Get-up-and-go attitude, energetic, empowered, speedy, driven, inventive, and resourceful

Option 2: Unsure, unclear, lethargic, slow, idle, and resistant

If you have a pulse, I am guessing you chose Option 1. In my experience, however, too many new philanthropic efforts crawl out of the gate because the participants and leaders are operating at Option 2. They don't take initiative. But it's relatively simple to set and elevate expectations for initiative taking.

In my consulting practice, my team uses the "Five Degrees of Initiative" originally proposed in a *Harvard Business Review Classics* article, "Who's Got the Monkey?" by William Oncken and Donald Wass. **The Five Degrees are:**

1. Waiting to be told what to do

2. Asking what to do

3. Making a recommendation, getting approval, and then taking the recommended action

4. Taking action, but advising Putnam at once

5. Acting on your own, then routinely reporting to Putnam

I have found it is in my clients' best interest for my team to be working at Levels 4 and 5 as much as possible, and sometimes at Level 3. We also know that there are many occasions when this is not possible and that moving down to Level 3 or even Level 2 is required. But it is rarely acceptable to be at Level 1.

Foundation leaders can use this simple list to talk about the expectations of initiative participants and set the bar at Levels 4 and 5 as much as possible. You can also give examples of what constitutes a Level 4 decision, and when you should stick to Level 2. The more initiative your team feels empowered to take, the faster you will achieve results. Guaranteed.

●　　●　　●

DO YOUR HOMEWORK TO INCREASE GRANTMAKING SUCCESS

Many foundations pour money down the drain by launching new funding guidelines and grant programs without first doing their homework. When funders develop new grantmaking strategies, they should dedicate time and resources to understanding the needs of the issue or population they want to help, identifying best practices and models that are already demonstrating success, and finding the right partners to help them succeed. Here are the minimum seven things you should learn:

1. **Understand current needs and challenges.** You need to understand the scope and scale of the problem, whether it's gang violence, access to health care, poor-quality after-school programs, or inadequate workforce development. How many and what types of people are affected? What impact is this having right now on families, communities, health care centers, or the local economy? Where, geographically, is this problem the greatest? What data is available to inform

your understanding, or what data might you want to collect? For example, the Cleveland Foundation wanted to build on the success of its early childhood initiative and support development among older youth. It explored the local community's knowledge about the needs of young people ages 6 to 24. The foundation also pulled data from local universities, public agencies, school districts, and nonprofits to examine the numbers around specific problems such as teen pregnancy, gang involvement, youth unemployment, and high school dropout rates. It used that data to identify cities and neighborhoods that had the greatest needs, then talked with leaders at various levels to better understand problems related to systems coordination, policy barriers, program quality, and nonprofit capacity. Armed with this data, it engaged hundreds of community stakeholders in conversations to analyze the information and prioritize needs. As a result, the foundation launched a clearly targeted youth development initiative that leveraged more than $15 million in additional philanthropic, city, county, and federal funding in its first five years.

2. **Anticipate future needs.** You also need to look ahead and anticipate what is likely to happen if the problem continues unchecked. What will it mean for your city's workforce ten years from now if high school graduation rates continue to hover at 60 percent? What will happen to the local arts community—an important source of tourism and revenue—if there is a dearth of leadership in the arts? For example, Northern California Grantmakers realized that the nonprofit and philanthropic sector in the San Francisco Bay Area was not adequately prepared to continue operations and respond in the event of a major disaster, such as a large earthquake. It responded by convening a Disaster Planning Task Force of member foundations, and with the help of a consultant conducted a needs assessment

and developed a strategic plan to educate and organize foundations to prepare for, respond to, and recover from a major local disaster.

3. **Build on strengths.** A mistake most funders make is to focus only on problems. You also need to understand what's working in your community. What are the strengths you can build upon? In the field of social work, this referred to as a "strengths perspective" rather than a "deficit approach." Your strategies should help strengthen and expand what's working well and build on your community's assets. Strengths and opportunities could exist in any area you're working on: a recent change in city government that opens the door for new partnerships; neighborhood leaders who are making a difference largely "under the radar" of foundations, nonprofits, and government agencies; certain organizations whose success rates are off the charts; existing networks of nonprofit leaders; etc.

4. **Determine your focus.** After you investigate current needs, challenges, and strengths, you will likely have an overwhelming number of options that your foundation could pursue. At this stage it's important to begin pruning these down to the one, two, or three ideas that are the most compelling, most in alignment with your foundation's mission and culture, and most manageable to implement. When the Charles and Helen Schwab Foundation explored opportunities to increase economic development and reduce poverty, it examined a range of strategies including savings and asset building, micro-enterprise development, employment, and workforce development, as well as strategies focused specifically on reducing poverty among women and girls. Ultimately it chose asset development and employment and support for working families as the areas in which it could create the greatest impact.

5. **Identify best practices and darned good ideas.** You don't want to reinvent the wheel. You do want to learn from others' success and see if there are strategies you can effectively replicate. Yes, they will need to be adapted to meet the needs of your community, but that's a lot easier than creating the whole thing from scratch. You can identify "best practices" (which have been thoroughly evaluated and determined to be effective), "promising practices" (evaluation is underway and the early results appear to demonstrate success) and "darned good ideas" (ideas that seem fabulous and worth trying, even if they're untested). In the case of the Cleveland Foundation's youth development initiative, the foundation examined national best practices such as engaging youth voice and leadership in designing and implementing the initiative, incorporating nationally accepted youth development principles, and using nationally tested program quality-assessment tools and outcomes tracking software.

6. **Find resources and partners.** With any issue, in any community, and at any scale, there are people, organizations, and other resources (e.g., money, data, materials) that can help you succeed. Ask yourself: What experts can join our advisory group? What data are already being collected? What organizations (schools, universities, corporations, government agencies, other foundations, etc.) would make good partners? What nonprofits are leading in this area? What other foundations are supporting this issue?

7. **Know how you'll learn.** Decide how you will learn and improve. Put processes in place to course-correct as needed. A formal evaluation method is one way, but you can also convene colleagues, grantees, and stakeholders to check in on progress, identify challenges and opportunities, and determine whether any changes should be made.

These seven steps may sound like a lot of work. They can be—and, honestly, they should be. The "homework" you complete up front can save you from heartburn (and potential heartbreak) down the road. You'll save yourself and everyone else involved hours of wasted time and energy. Best of all, these steps cost virtually nothing—just time spent reading, questioning, talking, and listening—and will steer your foundation's precious philanthropic resources toward the most effective uses.

To get started, review these steps with fellow staff members and consultants. Generate conversations about what they could mean for your next project. Then create a plan for incorporating them into your next grantmaking initiative, and watch as your effectiveness grows!

●　●　●

TEN WAYS TO SHAPE YOUR FOUNDATION'S NEWEST GRANTMAKING INITIATIVE

One reason we are involved in grantmaking is to be a part of making local, state, national, and global change from the ground up. Grantmakers often see real need for change in programs and services, or they see places where a new approach will make all the difference. The key to creating real change is understanding and preparing for the complexities of a grantmaking initiative before diving in.

Careful planning, focused relationship building, and a little thirst for adventure can help you take your next grantmaking initiative to new heights while respecting the boundaries of budgets, staff, and other limited resources. **Here are ten tips on getting started with your next initiative:**

1. **Anticipate ongoing complexity.** Grantmaking initiatives often spring from an idea brought to the table with a lot of enthusiasm. "We can curb obesity in our community if we restructure our neighborhoods to be easily walkable." Sounds simple enough. But grantmaking initiatives are rarely simple. They require many moving parts that can shift direction quickly. Suddenly you realize you need more funders, more partners, more energy, and more ideas. Be prepared for the inevitable roadblocks so you can generate the necessary support.

2. **Lock in leadership support.** Make sure that you have the full and unwavering support of the sponsoring foundation's leadership and board before embarking on any initiative. Confirm that there will be follow-through from beginning to end, and that leadership will remain supportive and engaged throughout the initiative. The support will prove invaluable—if not imperative— throughout the initiative's life span.

3. **Dedicate management capacity.** A strong, resourceful manager who is willing to lead the charge is vital to the success of any initiative. You need someone who is both enthusiastic and fully engaged in the effort you are embarking on, and who has the skill sets and knowledge to build relationships and oversee the process. Once the initiative is underway, be sure to continue to provide the administrative and task-focused support needed, so he or she can stay focused on the big picture.

4. **Engage foundation staff.** A new initiative may be the spark your foundation needs to ignite fresh energy among staff members. Although you want one person to be the point man (or woman), tap into your existing staff to see where their skills may best be used to support the new project. They may be excited

to manage some relationships, sustain and generate communications, design evaluations, and raise funds. Foundation staff can also pitch in to review proposals and conduct site visits.

5. **Allow ample time.** A strong and strategic grantmaking initiative is not developed overnight. Make sure you allow time for planning, relationship building, and stakeholder engagement. Take time to design a strong initiative before launching it. Then develop a theory of change to ensure that you can continue to articulate your goals and strategies throughout the initiative to guide ongoing management and evaluation.

6. **Build strong relationships.** Determine who needs to be involved and, equally important, who wants to be involved. A partner with a passion for your work is as valuable or even more valuable than a partner with a pocketbook but no passion. In any successful initiative, a lot of relationship building goes on behind the scenes. Use in-person meetings and phone conferences to engage partners, build momentum, address concerns, and put out fires. Let administrative staff manage the scheduling so that you and your key players can manage the relationships.

7. **Cultivate ongoing communications.** Internal and external communications are vital to the success of any initiative. Use your communications staff or key partners if they're available. Otherwise, retain outside experts to identify audiences, hone key messages, and craft a communications plan. Stakeholders and key audiences must be able to clearly and consistently communicate the goals of the initiative at every stage of its development. Make sure your communications complement your initiative. If you are funding arts in schools, be creative; if you are funding an environmental program, be green.

8. Meet pressure with action. Foundation staff often are pressured to make initiative grants quickly, far before planning is complete. Understandably, the foundation board wants to ensure that every dollar has a positive impact, while still demonstrating that the initiative's funds are being invested in the appropriate communities or agencies. Anticipate this pressure by planning in advance for initiative success. Small pilot grants can be made during the planning stage to test the waters before launching the fully developed initiative.

9. Embrace risk! Any initiative or change effort involves risk. Be brave! Name the risks and embrace them. Have the initiative planning team brainstorm a "risk list." What might this list include? Perhaps funding did not have the impact anticipated, or you incurred negative PR where you anticipated a positive reaction. Discuss strategies to mitigate each risk. Bring the risk list to each planning meeting for review and updating. Some risks will disappear, and new ones will become evident. Remember: In community grantmaking, taking risks is often a vital part of creating solutions.

10. Remember that the foundation is on the line. Launching an initiative takes a major commitment from a foundation. Keep in mind that the initiative's success or failure will reflect directly back onto the foundation itself. Embrace risk, yes, but also leverage all available resources to ensure success. The CEO or board chair might serve as an initiative champion. Top leadership could make key introductions to business, political, and community leaders. With strong support from the inside out, a well-planned initiative can generate years of positive impact.

Developing a new initiative from vision to implementation can be a challenge, but the rewards of a successful endeavor far outweigh the difficulties. Maybe you have an initiative in mind that you would like to bring to your board. Start your planning today, so you are fully armed with answers when questions start coming to you. Who are your potential partners? What are your goals, and what barriers might get in the way of achieving them? How does the initiative reflect the mission of your foundation? Answer these questions now and you will be on your way to making an investment that makes all the difference, in the near term and in the future.

●　　●　　●

ONE QUESTION GUARANTEED TO SAVE FUNDERS TIME AND MONEY —AND ACHIEVE RESULTS

In my experience, the most effective foundations do one thing without fail: They ask the question guaranteed to save time and money and to achieve results. That question is this: "If you could do it all over again, what would you do differently?"

If you ask that question of your grantees, other organizations working on the same issue, and other foundations that have attempted to do what you're trying to do, I guarantee you will reap the benefits. Listen to what they have to say, implement their suggestions, and you will save your foundation staff time, financial resources, and headaches. You will also have a much more successful grantmaking program, and it will happen much faster than if you hadn't asked the question.

Here are a few times when asking, "If you could do it all over again, what would you do differently?" will help you. **Ask this question when you are:**

- Conducting an environmental scan to plan your next funding initiative (you could ask this of other communities, other funders, nonprofits, potential grantees).

- Determining the best approach to evaluating your grant portfolio and what qualities to look for in an evaluator (you might ask this of other funders who have conducted evaluations of similar portfolios or of similarly complex funding efforts).
- Assessing the impact of your grantmaking strategy and determining what a phase two might look like (you could ask your grantees, partners, stakeholders, and even your own staff).
- Improving your foundation's organizational practices, such as how you review grant proposals, communicate with grantees, become a Lean organization, or improve your customer service (you could ask this of your staff, and of other foundations who have undertaken similar improvement efforts).

It's simple, right? Ask the question, listen to the answers, implement the suggestions, save yourself time and resources, get faster results, and have greater impact. I guarantee it works.

● ● ●

SUCCESSFUL RFP MANAGEMENT: TEN TIPS TO SELECT THE BEST GRANTEES

The RFP is essential to the way many organizations make grants, so improvements in the RFP process can have a profound impact on grantmaking success. We have helped many foundations and corporate grantmakers develop and manage requests for proposals as they identify the best nonprofits to fund. Over the years, my experience and research have revealed these ten steps a funder can take to help make RFPs successful.

1. Be crystal clear on what you want to accomplish with your funding initiative.

This means understanding your vision, your mission, your objectives and strategies, and what dollar amount you want to use to achieve your goals.

2. **Envision your ideal applicants.** Who do you want to apply for this funding initiative? What kind of organizations? What skill level and experience do they need to have? Do you want an organization that has been doing this work for a long time—one you can take to the next level—or are you seeking to fund a start-up?

3. **Put customer service first.** You have two main customers here. The first is the beneficiary (the person, family, or community that your grantees seek to help); be sure that your approach is of greatest value to that person or group. The second customer is the nonprofit organizations that will be responding to your RFP. Treat them like customers, not like servants; don't make them jump through unnecessary hoops or give them unrealistic deadlines.

4. **Conduct significant outreach to potential applicants.** Your methods may vary depending on whether your RFP is open, meaning anybody can apply, or whether it is by invitation only. If it's an open RFP, how will your ideal applicant learn about it—what networks and associations can help you disseminate the RFP? The critical issue is ensuring that the applicants you want to apply are aware of the RFP in time to actually submit their proposals. Of course, you face similar issues even with a closed RFP: You might need to do some initial research to find the best nonprofits to invite, and they too will need plenty of time to apply.

5. **Get honest feedback from people outside your organization.** Share a draft of the RFP with executive directors of organizations similar to your ideal applicant or with funder colleagues from other foundations. Give

them permission to give you honest feedback, including criticism that tests your assumptions. You don't want to solicit feedback from people who will just tell you that everything looks great.

6. **Determine your staffing needs in advance.** You want to think about what resources you're going to need, how to plan and develop them, who will write the RFP, how many proposals you anticipate, and how many people you will need to help you review the proposals. Will you need staff to conduct site visits? How will other people in your organization be involved or impacted? Staff from grants management, communications, and evaluation may all need to be involved in reviewing proposals, so you'll want to think through a plan for engaging all these individuals to help you successfully implement your RFP.

7. **Develop your review criteria before issuing the RFP.** This might seem unnecessary now, because of course it will be a while before you're actually reviewing proposals. But it can be helpful and efficient to think about this early on. When those proposals come in, how are you going to review them? Not just in terms of the staffing discussed above, but in terms of what your criteria will be. For example, will you use a scoring system? By developing your review criteria in advance, you can identify gaps and areas of confusion or duplication in your RFP—and correct them—before you disseminate it.

8. **Anticipate your expectations for grantee involvement in the funding initiative.** Will there be an evaluation? If so, what data-collection needs will you have? Are there expectations that your grantee will be convened regularly or will participate in a learning community? If so, how do you make sure these expectations are clear to the applicants before they apply?

9. **Anticipate applicant questions and prepare answers to frequently asked questions (FAQs).** Consider in advance what kinds of questions your applicants may have and where there might be areas of confusion. For example, do terms need to be clarified? I recommend actually creating an FAQs document in advance and issuing it when the RFP is released; then you can update it as needed, as applicant questions start coming in.

10. **Debrief once the dust settles.** After you've reviewed the proposals, made funding decisions, issued the grant, and disseminated your press release, take some time to reflect on the process. What could have gone better? What worked well? What would you do differently? Ideally, ask for perspectives from applicants who were declined as well as the grantees that you funded. Make sure you document what you learn and share it with your colleagues at your foundation. And don't forget to refer to it the next time you develop an RFP, to make sure that you've retained the lessons you've learned throughout this process.

Using even a few of these tips will benefit your grantmaking program, but obviously all of them work together and build on one another. As you begin to apply these ideas to your RFP process, they will become a seamless part of your grantmaking and ultimately will make a profound impact. My best clients leverage all ten of these points to ensure that their RFPs create the most successful grantmaking programs for their foundations.

● ● ●

SIX SIGNS YOUR FUNDING INITIATIVE IS IN TROUBLE

I have helped dozens of foundations explore, develop, and launch new grantmaking programs and initiatives. In my experience there are six red flags indicating trouble ahead. If you are experiencing any of these, now is the time to intervene. Investments made now will be easier and less costly than trying to resurrect a failing initiative later. **Here are six signs to watch out for:**

1. **You aren't evaluating your impact.** There is an initial period of time when key stakeholders buy into your strategy out of good will and belief that because you are trying to, you will make a difference. But that good will has a shelf life. Stories are important, but quantitative and qualitative evidence must demonstrate success over time. Your funding partners and coalition members will start to fall off if they do not feel that they are investing time and resources in something that demonstrates value. Even if you are several years into your project, it's not too late to conduct a retrospective evaluation and get back on track.

2. **Your evaluation results show little or no impact.** While it takes a while to show results, especially when you're trying to tackle complex problems such as ending homelessness, developing communities, and reducing chronic absenteeism in schools, if your results demonstrate you aren't making a difference, it's time to regroup. It might be that your assumptions and strategies should change, you aren't investing enough resources, or you aren't investing resources in the right things. It could even mean that your evaluation design is simply not capturing the early and intermediate wins.

Whatever the case, you need to fix it.

3. **You have no communications plan.** I've said it before and I will say it again: Communication is critical for the success of grantmaking initiatives. This includes internal communication (your team, funders, and close stakeholders) and external communication (everyone else who can influence or who has a stake in what you're doing). If you don't prioritize communications planning now—and I do mean right now—you're going to pay the price in a year (or five or ten years) when your grantees and partners aren't coordinated and are unable to stay on the same page, and stakeholders and other funders are confused by what you're trying to do.

4. **Key stakeholders don't understand what you are doing.** When you hear your partners and funders saying things like, "Yes, we are involved, but we really don't know what they are trying to do" or "I've read the Theory of Change three times and I still don't get it," you need some help. You might need to improve communications (you have a clear plan but you aren't articulating it well), find better ways to engage key funders and partners, or revisit your strategies. Maybe you are trying to accomplish too much too quickly and need to scale back. Whatever the solution, you need to act soon or these partners will start dropping off.

5. **Initiative leadership is "off topic" or, worse, has another agenda.** Chances are you have brought on someone else to lead this initiative—an intermediary, a consultant, a grantee, or a national program office. Without micromanaging, you need to make sure they are clearly advancing your mission and your goals for this initiative.

6. **You aren't trusting your instincts.** If your gut feeling is that something is off, the person you hired isn't the right fit, or that key leaders have concerns but aren't expressing them—you need to follow your instinct. Chances are you are right. If not, you can put your worries to rest. If you notice that you are talking yourself out of your concerns ("But she is so qualified and everyone liked her in the interview," "We don't have time to make changes right now," "There must be a reason he won't return my calls; I'm sure he's busy"), act quickly. Identify a few trusted colleagues and talk to them individually and confidentially to gain perspective.

If one of these warning signs applies to you, you need to make some course corrections quickly. If two or three are relevant, your initiative is heading for trouble. If you are experiencing five to six of them, you need an immediate intervention. The people and communities you seek to help are too important to let your great ideas and efforts go down the drain. Yes, you have a lot on your plate today, but the time you spend immediately to confirm and tackle these problems will pay off exponentially.

THE MOST EFFECTIVE FOUNDATIONS
DO ONE THING WITHOUT FAIL: THEY
ASK THEMSELVES THE QUESTION
GUARANTEED TO SAVE TIME AND MONEY,
AND ACHIEVE RESULTS.

Management
and Operations

SIMPLICITY AND SUCCESS: THREE WAYS TO REDUCE LABOR INTENSITY

Grantmakers, and their consultants, tend to overcomplicate things. Let me give you two simple examples of how this wastes time and prevents success.

First example: Biweekly meetings. I've worked for funders who wanted me to stage biweekly meetings, for groups both large and small. In all cases, the process came before the goal: Each funder decided to have biweekly meetings before thinking about what they really wanted to accomplish. How effective the meetings were in reaching the goal was not a consideration.

Second example: One-year grants. Offering a year of funding sounds fiscally responsible, since you're checking for success before funding another year. But if you're really likely to keep funding this organization, aren't you being fiscally irresponsible? Think about the time the grantees spend writing proposals and reports; their staff's inability to plan long term, their need to come up with contingency plans, and their stress level; the organization's need to focus on the budget while waiting for the next grant approval. For a $25,000 grant, the nonprofit probably spends at least $5,000 in time on their proposal—and your program officers, board, and grant managers probably spent that much again in time for reviews, write-ups, decision making, and processing. That $20,000 grant might easily cost $10,000.

So let's look at three concrete things you can do to reduce your labor intensity.

1. Assume that your process is flawed. Don't automatically accept the standard way of doing what you do. Ask yourselves, "Why are we doing it this way?" and "How can we reduce the labor intensity on this project?"

2. Identify three alternatives. Come up with three different options and try them out. Remember those biweekly meetings? Maybe a better plan is to bring everyone together for a well-facilitated one-day meeting, where you can make decisions and move on. Or you could conduct some research first, then let your group make informed choices based on your findings. Or you could just meet monthly, with an email update in between.

3. Figure out the staff costs. Guesstimate the annual salary and benefits of everyone involved. Divide by 2,080 hours (the number of working hours per year) and calculate everyone's hourly rate. Then add those up and decide if that cost is worth it. Whether it costs a collective $10,000 for everyone to join biweekly phone calls all year long, perhaps you'd rather spend $10,000 on flying everyone to meet for a day with a facilitator to come to some decisions, so that you can spend the rest of the year implementing rather than meeting.

And with all that spare time you'll gain, go for a walk, play with your kids, take a nap, relax. . . . You deserve it!

GRANTMAKERS SHOULD THINK LIKE CONSULTANTS

I believe foundations could save time, solve problems more efficiently, and add greater value if their senior leadership would think like consultants.

Let me explain: Most consultants work on a time-and-materials basis, meaning that they have an hourly rate. Foundation leaders who hire those consultants deem the value of their work worth that fee. However, foundation leaders rarely calculate the cost and value of their own staff's time—which is a pretty simple thing to do.

Let's say the annual salary of a senior program officer at your foundation is $100,000. Let's assume her annual benefits are 25 percent, so now you are at $125,000. There are 2,080 working hours per year, so if you divide $125,000 by 2,080 hours, you'll have $60 per hour.

Now think about some of the activities your senior program officer is expected to do. A weekly two-hour staff meeting for 50 weeks a year would be $6,000. Spending two weeks preparing board dockets (participating in meetings, writing and rewriting board materials for your docket deadline) is $4,800. If you do this every quarter, that's $19,200 for your one senior program officer. Conducting mandatory site visits for 25 grantees a year? That could be $12,000 if you assume it takes eight hours to plan, prepare, travel, conduct, and summarize each site visit.

What are the costs for all of your staff to engage in these activities? You can begin to see how it adds up. Of course your staff needs to meet regularly, you need to conduct site visits, and you need to prepare for board meetings. **But consider the value your foundation is receiving for your staff to engage in all of these activities by asking yourself these four questions:**

1. What is the value we're getting for the cost?

2. Is the value worth this cost?

3. Are there ways we can increase the value of this activity?

4. Are there ways we can be more efficient with our time?

I'm positive that if you think about your staff's time versus the value you receive, you'll be surprised, and you'll come up with some creative ways to accomplish more with the human capital that you have.

● ● ●
STOP THE BOARD DOCKET MADNESS

Every year, and generally every quarter, tens of thousands of foundations and their staff go into a frenzy of activity preparing for board meetings. They prepare binders of carefully scripted summaries of the grants they're recommending for approval. These involve layers of bureaucratic approval processes, PowerPoint presentations, page lengths, word counts, and wordsmithing.

I have clients who warn me in advance that they will not be available for two full weeks before their board meeting deadlines. Then they spend another half week on the actual board meeting, and finally they spend the next week catching up on emails, voicemails, and meetings they couldn't get to during the previous weeks.

That's three and a half weeks in which these foundation executives have no time to think, be creative, work on bigger-picture issues, or build relationships or solve problems.

It's also three and a half weeks when their grantees, consultants, and partners have to go into a holding pattern.

And the truly terrifying part of this is that it happens four times a year.

Here are five things you can do to reduce the labor intensity of your board meetings:

1. **Clarify the goals of your board meetings.** What are the top three things you want to accomplish? List them, then identify the most efficient ways to accomplish them.

2. **Calculate the actual staff time and cost of each board meeting.** Ask a subset of your staff to jot down all of the time they spend directly preparing for or participating in the next two board meetings, and how. They should include team meetings to vet projects, write-ups, rehearsals, etc. Involve a cross section of your staff so that you have an idea of the time spent by program officers, associates, administrative assistants, finance, and communications staff.

3. **Ask staff for their opinions.** I can guarantee that they have opinions about board meetings and board dockets, and they probably have some great ideas for making them more efficient and less exhausting. Discuss the best ideas and prioritize them.

4. **Ask your board for ideas.** These are busy people who want to make sure that their time is spent well—and who have a fiduciary responsibility to make sure your staff and foundation are adequately allocating time and resources.

Generate creative solutions. Maybe you could hold three board meetings a year instead of four. Perhaps you need only bring bigger grants and initiatives to your board for approval. Or you could allow for multi-year grants that the board doesn't have to approve annually.

The bottom line is this: The best foundations I know reduce their board docket madness to the bare minimum.

● ● ●

HOW WILL YOU SOLVE TOMORROW'S PROBLEMS?

By 2025, at least one-fifth of all grantmaking will focus on solving problems that do not currently exist today or that we aren't yet aware of. Solving these problems will mean:

- Using data that has not yet been collected
- Applying technologies that have not been created or thought about thus far
- Engaging a workforce in jobs that do not currently exist

If you don't believe me, consider some of today's problems that we weren't aware of ten years ago:

- Ebola: Ten years ago no one thought we would be concerned about an Ebola outbreak in the United States.
- Substance abuse: Overdose deaths from prescription painkillers have skyrocketed in the past decade, and kids can now buy synthetic marijuana at their local mall (it's marketed as incense).
- Toxic chemicals: We are exposed to an increasing amount of toxic chemicals. Most of us weren't checking labels for BPA-free plastic ten years ago. Today's children are born with more than 200 toxic chemicals in their umbilical cord blood.
- Early math: There is mounting evidence that the mathematical understanding of preschoolers is highly

predictive of how well they will do in math and other subjects, and kids who lack this knowledge when they start school typically do not catch up. I'm a mom of two preschoolers and I didn't even realize this. This is a problem because more than half of three- and four-year-olds in the United States do not attend preschool.

To be positioned to identify and tackle tomorrow's problems, there are four questions grantmakers should ask themselves:

- Are we continually scanning the field, community, and environment in each of our program areas?
- In what ways do we regularly expose ourselves to new ideas and thinking?
- Do we regularly review our human capital and leadership, and make strategic investments in their development?
- Do we intentionally stay abreast of technology and identify ways to leverage it?

While you think about those, I'm going to go play some math games with my preschool twins.

BY 2025, AT LEAST ONE-FIFTH OF ALL GRANTMAKING WILL FOCUS ON SOLVING PROBLEMS THAT DO NOT CURRENTLY EXIST TODAY OR THAT WE AREN'T YET AWARE OF.

Customer Service

• • • WHO IS YOUR CUSTOMER?

It's easy to get mired in the way things have always been done, and sometimes it leaves us blind to our customers' real needs. So take a moment and ask yourself one critical question: Who is my customer? In my experience, this is a question that most foundations simply don't ask themselves.

I was talking last week with a funder client (let's call her Mary) who said that a big lesson she learned is that they should give their applicants more time to respond to a request for proposal. They had only given their applicants about a month; during that month, the applicant had to decide whether and how to apply jointly with other organizations that were also invited, prepare the application, secure matching funding, and write the proposal.

Nonprofits are essentially this foundation's clients, and it was obvious to me that they were asking their customers to scramble to do all of this in a very short period of time. Actually, the fact that Mary was surprised to learn that a month was not enough time to make all of that happen was what surprised me. This seems like the kind of learning that one would expect from someone new to philanthropy, or perhaps from a relatively new foundation with little grantmaking experience. But this foundation has been in existence for literally decades, awarding hundreds of millions of dollars in grants every year. As an organization, they have likely issued close to a thousand requests for proposals over their decades of existence.

When I asked Mary why they had such a tight time line, she explained all the various departments and people within the foundation who had to sign off and approve a request for proposals: communications staff, grant management staff, contracting, finance. There were multiple levels of leadership, and each of them had a week to review the RFP before passing it on to the next person within the bureaucracy.

When you added up all the time they gave themselves internally to approve RFPs, it was significantly more time than the applicants were given to apply. The trouble is that they weren't paying attention to their customers. Are they there to serve themselves, or are they there to help nonprofit organizations have an impact on the issues they care about?

By contrast, another client we work with has spent tremendous time and resources to re-engineer their internal processes, increase automation, become more internally lean, and speed up decision making in order to increase efficiency and better serve their grantees. I believe they do this because they recognize that the grantees are their customers, and they focus on themselves only to discover how they can better support their grantees.

Three questions can help get to the heart of the matter:

- Who is your customer? Your staff, or the nonprofit partners you are funding to meet the goals of your foundation?
- Are you aware of what your grantees are experiencing in trying to work with you?
- What steps can you as a foundation take to examine your internal processes and determine whether your focus is on helping yourselves or on helping the communities of the nonprofits that you serve?

The answers to these three questions should provide insight into your grantmaking practices. I hope you will spend some time considering and discussing your answers, because doing so should provide a clear road map to improved customer service—with the ultimate goal of better grantmaking.

●   ●   ●

UBER PHILANTHROPY

I am a recent user and fan of Uber, an app that allows you to immediately find a car service, visually track the car, communicate with the driver, and pay remotely. It's easy, reliable, fast, and consumer-driven.

I think philanthropy leaders can learn from Uber about how to innovate for greater impact. It's all about taking a standard practice we take for granted, turning it on its head, and radically improving the customer experience.

That's what Uber did. We've all stood on street corners watching taxi after taxi drive by, wondering when and if one would ever become available. Uber took the obvious (a stressful, risky, and inefficient mode of transportation) and created a radically different customer experience (you select the type of car you want, tap a few buttons to request a car, it is available within minutes, you can communicate directly with the driver, you can watch his or her progress on a map on your phone, and you don't need cash or credit card in hand). Similarly, philanthropy leaders can identify practices we all take for granted and brainstorm how they could be turned on their heads to make them better, faster, smarter, easier, more impactful.

For example:

- **Nonprofits write proposals to receive funding—** What if funders had to make the case to nonprofits to accept their money and participate in their initiative?
- **Grantseekers remain in the dark about their proposal status until the foundation decides to share information—**What if there was an online proposal tracking system so that at any moment, the grantseeker could click a button and identify the exact stage of proposal review?
- **Program officers bring all the expertise and "inside baseball" knowledge, and therefore they select grantees—**What if grantees selected program officers, or community experts offered just-in-time advice on all funding decisions?

I realize there are potential challenges with all of those ideas above. But before you pull out your fire hoses and turn them on me, acknowledge this: As funders, we like to tell nonprofits that they need to innovate. But when is the last time we truly tried to innovate our own long-standing practices? We all can creatively rethink what we take for granted, and turn those processes on their heads for greater efficiency and impact.

ARE WE KILLING THE MAGIC?

On a recent trip with my twins to Magic Kingdom at Disney World, I was taken aback by the multiple barriers to actually entering the park, and the disappointing experience leaving the park after a fabulous, fun-filled day. Yes, it was fun while we were there, but the lead-up and send-off essentially killed the Magic Kingdom's "magic" for me.

It got me thinking: What roadblocks do foundations inadvertently create, preventing ideal applicants from applying and great ideas from being funded? What opportunities are lost at the end of a grant period? How can we make sure we're not killing the "magic" that comes from a synergistic and mutually fulfilling foundation-grantee relationship?

Let me explain how the magic gets killed. On our way to Magic Kingdom, we had to deal with seven barriers to entry before we could actually enter the park. **We had to:**

1. Wait at the parking tollbooth and pay for parking.

2. Wait in line for the free shuttle to take us from the parking lot to what we thought was the park (it was actually the Disney "transportation center").

3. Figure out that we were not yet at Magic Kingdom, and either stand in line for what appeared to be a 45-minute wait to take the monorail or notice that there was a much shorter line to take a ferry.

4. Take the ferry to Magic Kingdom.

5. Wait in line to pick up our tickets at will call.

6. Wait in a separate line to have our bags checked.

7. Wait in yet another line to have our fingerprints scanned and linked to our Disney Pass.

It was a full hour from the time we paid for parking to the time we walked into the park, and it was not a busy day! At no time were Mickey, Minnie, Donald Duck, or Cinderella walking around to at least keep the kids entertained or remind us that we were actually in the wonderful world of Disney. Few staff were on hand to explain to overwhelmed parents whose children had to use the potty what was going on, where to go, or what to do. I imagine Disney spends billions of dollars per year on advertising to get families like ours to spend $360 in tickets to be there on a given day—so why make it so hard to walk in the door? We had fun, we rode rides, we had our pictures taken with princesses. But my most vivid memory was exiting the park at 5:00 p.m. (long before the park closed). The employees were gone, the ticket windows were closed. All you saw were gray cement structures. No Mickey Mouse waved good-bye, no signs bid us to come back real soon, nothing reminded us of what a wonderful time we had just had, no incentive encouraged us to visit other Disney parks. Nothing.

Foundations are well positioned to wrap a meaningful and memorable experience around their grant distributions. Yet, intentionally or unintentionally, they repeatedly set up roadblocks that make it difficult for great ideas and great nonprofits to be funded, or they leave grantees amid the tumbleweeds once a grant is finished.

Here are just 10 of the dozens of barriers to entry that I have seen:

1. No information available about the foundation or its guidelines

2. Vague funding guidelines

3. Lack of contact information for foundation staff on websites

4. Messages clearly stating, "We don't accept unsolicited proposals"

5. Refusing to discuss project ideas with nonprofits

6. Lack of communication with grantseekers once proposals are submitted

7. Unanswered emails and unreturned voice mails

8. Requiring applicants to obtain matching funds within three weeks in order to submit a proposal

9. Working with an applicant on a proposal for six months and then telling them they aren't going to fund it because their priorities have changed

10. Using proposals as a way to surface new ideas, but not funding them

And similar to my Disney experience, the end of the grant period can be lackluster and a lost opportunity for learning, creativity, and expansion. Here is what typically happens: Toward the end of grant, the foundation's grants management system sends an automated message to the grantee that their final report is due. The grantee fills out the report and mails it in. The program officer is too busy to read it, and it gets filed with the grants management system. The grantee can apply again if they want to (although some foundations require they wait three months to a year to reapply). No conversation. No real learning about what worked, what didn't, what challenges or opportunities the nonprofit learned that could be shared with the funder. No brainstorming new ways that the nonprofit and foundation could partner. No sharing with the nonprofit the names of other funders it might pursue. The funder-nonprofit relationship simply ends, and all the energy originally exerted to bring both parties together just dissipates.

As grantmakers, we should honestly count how many barriers we create that prevent grantseekers from applying for funds or sharing good ideas with us. Then we should ask ourselves what messages these barriers send; which can be eliminated or reduced; and how we can be more welcoming, transparent, responsive, and encouraging. Similarly, we should think of our relationship with the nonprofits we fund as a relationship, with mutual learning and sharing, and value for both organizations beyond the grant itself and beyond the grant period.

In other words, we should look for every opportunity to keep the magic alive.

●　　●　　●

ONE SMALL STEP GOES A LONG WAY IN THE PHILANTHROPIC "CUSTOMER EXPERIENCE"

When I stayed at the Charles Hotel near Harvard Square, I was delighted to see the "Web Cube" on my hallway on my way to my room. That's essentially a large closet with a desk, computer, printer, and free Internet access, available to all guests on the floor. I assume each floor has them. What a brilliant improvement to an existing valuable resource: hotel business centers.

We've all used hotel business centers and have encountered similar problems: finding them, using them during limited business hours, and planning our time so that we don't have to go back and forth from our room to the business center and back. This Web Cube takes the customer experience to a new level. If you are busy working in your hotel room and want to print something so that you can go back to your room to use it, just walk a few yards down your hallway. If you are under deadline and working late at night or waking up, as I often do, at 3:00 a.m. with the urge to finish that project, you could probably use the Web Cube in your pajamas!

What was crystal clear to me was that the Charles Hotel understood that I was in Boston to do more than sleep. While a bed was my most basic need, I could tell that the staff at this hotel thought further about what their guests might be trying to accomplish and how they could support that as part of the hotel experience.

This makes me think about what we as philanthropists can do to improve the service and value we provide. What can we do to better understand and support what our grantees are trying to accomplish, and how might we improve our services to make them, and ourselves, more effective?

Think about one thing you or your foundation offers that others find valuable. This could be in-person workshops for grantees to improve board effectiveness or evaluate impact, "meet the grantmaker" sessions you hold for nonprofits to meet your program officers, technical assistance you provide to grantees, or your super-duper new online application process.

Now brainstorm ways that you could make this:

- **Easier to use**
- **Accessible to more people**
- **Available 24 hours a day**
- **More valuable**

If you pay consultants to provide technical assistance to certain grantees, how about paying for "consultants on call," meaning consultants would hold virtual "office hours" and be available to advise the broader nonprofit community?

If you fill the room at your quarterly nonprofit board trainings, why not record the sessions via audio or video to make them available as downloadable podcasts or webinars? Upload them to the Foundation Center's Issue Lab and they will be instantly available to thousands of libraries worldwide.

If your online grant application and management system alerts grantseekers when the application has been received, decisions have been made, and reports are due, could you add features that show the applicant where it is in the review process at any given time (program officer review, peer review process, board vote, etc.) so that nonprofits don't feel their proposal went into a black hole? While you're at it, share tips on effective nonprofit management and links to upcoming professional development opportunities.

All of these ideas may well require a small additional investment of time or funds on your part. But think of how your investment will pay off in terms of grantee productivity or new learning. No doubt, the powers that be at the Charles Hotel did some sort of cost/benefit analysis before taking away precious floor space to devote to the Web Cube. Their investment is paying off in terms of happier, more productive customers—and yours will as well.

As for me, the next time I'm in Boston, I'm staying at the Charles!

TAKE A MOMENT AND ASK YOURSELF ONE CRITICAL QUESTION: WHO IS MY CUSTOMER? IN MY EXPERIENCE, THIS IS A QUESTION THAT MOST FOUNDATIONS SIMPLY DON'T ASK THEMSELVES.

Communications

WHAT ARE YOU COMMUNICATING?

While in Palm Beach, Florida, I had the wonderful opportunity to meet with and learn from 25 of the world's top consultants, culminating in a discussion and dinner with James Carville. He advised us to clearly communicate who we are in order to stand out from the crowd and "break through the clutter." **He asked us to consider five questions:**

- **What is your brand?**
- **What do you stand for?**
- **Are you authentic?**
- **Do others say consistent things about you?**
- **What can you do better than others?**

Coincidentally, I am currently advising a growing family foundation on the development of a communications plan. The questions Carville asked us consultants are the same ones funders should ask of themselves:

- Does our foundation have a clear brand identity?
- Do we know what we stand for as a foundation? Do we have clear goals and strategies? Can all of our staff and board easily describe them in a casual conversation?
- Are we authentic? Do we "walk our talk"? Would our grantees and funder colleagues describe us in the same ways that we describe ourselves?
- Do our key stakeholders say consistent things about our foundation? If we randomly selected some of our grantees and partners, would they similarly describe our brand, our goals?
- How does our foundation differentiate itself? What is unique to us?

You might know the answers to all of those questions, or some of them. Regardless, it would be interesting to ask these questions at your next senior management meeting. You will find the discussion illuminating, and you might learn it is time to strengthen your communication muscle.

● ● ●

THE POWER OF A COMMUNICATIONS PLAN

One of the most important—yet overlooked and underestimated—actions foundations can take to ensure the success of their grantmaking initiatives is to develop and implement a comprehensive communications plan. I've been helping foundations design and develop grantmaking programs for close to 15 years; based on that experience, I have found that when foundations fail to make communications a priority at the beginning, they are less likely to obtain the results they seek. Here's why.

A few years ago, I organized a series of site visits for a foundation client to learn how other funders in other cities design similar initiatives. Some of the best advice we received was that communications begins the moment you begin discussing your new initiative, so be sure to start planning a communications strategy immediately.

Unfortunately, my client didn't follow that advice—for reasons that are easy to understand. We've all been there. It is the beginning of your grantmaking program and you're in the middle of planning and launching, which feels like you're building a plane and flying it at the same time. There is a lot of pressure to get grants out the door, even though you know more research and development are needed. You're scrambling to assess needs, identify partners, get all the funding in place, and collect data. This means communications planning feels like a luxury—or at least something you can put off until the elusive "Phase 2."

Believe me, I get it. But I also guarantee you that if you don't focus on communications planning immediately, your effort will stumble and falter a few months or years from now when the people most involved lack coordination, and those you are trying to engage externally aren't sure of your goals.

The good news is there are three simple things you can do right now, whether you're at the beginning of your initiative or already midway through:

1. **Make communications a priority right now.** This really is as important as developing a strategy, writing your request for proposal, identifying potential grantees, and finding an evaluator. It needs to be on your list of must-haves and not on the "we'll get to it later" list. Even if your initiative is underway, it's not too late to begin prioritizing this. Don't know where to start? Keep reading.

2. **Identify and leverage your existing communications assets.** Look at the existing marketing and communications staff within your foundation as well as those associated with your existing partners and your potential grantees. What are they already doing and how can they be further engaged in this project right away? Down the road, you might want to retain a communications consultant, but right now you need smart communications professionals who can sit around the table to help you identify your communications needs, your key audiences, and your messages, and help you to begin developing a plan. Chances are, these people are already close at hand.

3. **Reach for the low hanging fruit in communication needs and opportunities.** I'll bet there are five or ten things you can do right now, even as you are developing a communications plan, that could quickly alleviate some of your communications needs. These could be relatively simple endeavors, such as developing fact sheets, a standard PowerPoint deck, talking points, or a newsletter. Or they could be a bit more time intensive, such as conducting a series of individual meetings with key stakeholders to update them on progress.

I guarantee that by beginning to prioritize communications now, regardless of where you are in your initiative, you will reap benefits and avoid troubles in the future. The three easy communication tactics we discussed—making communications a priority, identifying and leveraging your communications assets, and reaching for low-hanging fruit in communications opportunities—make up a terrific launching point. Implementing those tips now, in conjunction with beginning to develop a more comprehensive communications plan, will set you well on your way to ensuring the success of your grantmaking program.

THE FOUR DIMENSIONS OF A SUCCESSFUL COMMUNICATIONS PLAN

No one likes to feel left out or overlooked, and when key stakeholders feel that way, the results can be painful and long lasting. I once conducted a focus group of community leaders who expressed serious concerns about the lack of communication within a significant regional initiative. When I asked the group what could be done to fix this, another participant said something I'll never forget: "Communications need to be top down, bottom up, inside out, and all around." I think that sums up the components of an effective communications plan.

The next time you launch a new grantmaking program or initiative for any issue, think through these four aspects of your communication needs so that none of your key stakeholders feels overlooked.

Top down
Make sure there are strategies in place for those who are managing, governing, and funding the initiative to communicate regularly with all the organizations, grantees, and partners doing the work. Priorities may need to shift based on things that are beyond the control of the initiative, such as changes in the economy or in government. It's important for you to be as transparent as possible and to ensure that your partners can count on you for regular updates.

Bottom up
You want to be sure there are regular opportunities for everyone involved in the initiative—grantees, evaluators, vendors, and other stakeholders—to regularly communicate with the people managing the initiative. Use any method that works for you: monthly meetings, quarterly check-ins, regular conference calls, or whatever allows people to feel comfortable and bring up

issues or concerns as they emerge—rather than a month or a year later, when it's too late.

Inside out
Everyone involved in your program needs to be regularly communicating and coordinating with each other. If you're trying to create change within a community, it likely means that the people and organizations need to do things differently. They might need to coordinate their work better or make joint decisions, so you need to put systems in place to allow for that communication and coordination to happen.

All around
The final way to think about your communications needs is to think about what's all around you—in other words, external communications. Suppose you could draw a circle that encompassed you and your grantees and partners, then look outside that circle: Think about who is not involved but should be, who needs to know about what you're doing, whom you should be influencing, and who might be trying to work against you whom you should instead engage. Once you've identified those groups, think about what each needs to know and how you might best communicate that.

Resolving your communications challenges is one critical component of positioning your foundation for success. When it comes to communications, there is no silver-bullet solution. Instead, leveraging all of these dimensions— top down, bottom up, inside out, and all around—is the key to eradicating your communications challenges and successfully engaging all of your stakeholders.

ONE OF THE MOST IMPORTANT—
YET OVERLOOKED AND
UNDERESTIMATED—ACTIONS
FOUNDATIONS CAN TAKE
TO ENSURE THE SUCCESS
OF THEIR GRANTMAKING
INITIATIVES IS TO DEVELOP AND
IMPLEMENT A COMPREHENSIVE
COMMUNICATIONS PLAN.

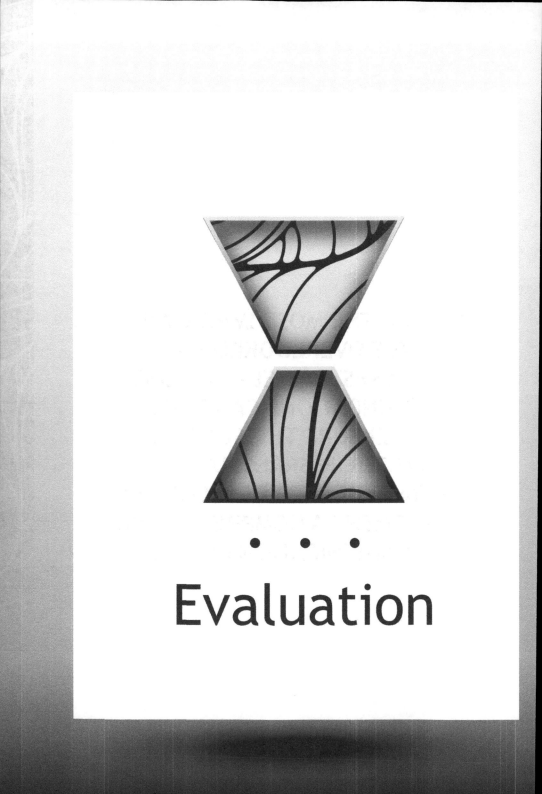

Evaluation

THE POWER OF TAKING STOCK: FIVE REASONS TO CONDUCT EVALUATIONS

Knowledge is power, as the saying goes, but I am not sure many foundations fully believe that. In the course of working with foundations across the country, I have made a somewhat surprising discovery: Many foundations grossly underestimate the importance of evaluating impact. This is unfortunate, because evaluation is both enlightening and empowering. In fact, measuring impact can give you power to ultimately increase that impact. **Here are five reasons why foundations should regularly conduct evaluations.**

1. Evaluate to measure impact.

The first reason to conduct evaluations is plain and simple: How will you know if you have had any influence unless you evaluate the effectiveness of your grantmaking program? There is really only one way to learn what the impact has been—and its scope and scale—and that is by conducting a thorough assessment and evaluation. Simply receiving anecdotal information or grant reports will not provide sufficient information to help you evaluate impact. A deeper evaluation and understanding is necessary, which leads us to the next four reasons.

2. Evaluate to discover unanticipated results.

Evaluations will often uncover consequences you might never have anticipated. For example, you might have a grant program that is designed to improve the leadership capacity of arts organizations in your community. In the course of conducting an evaluation to learn how leadership has improved, you might discover the following: As a result of your efforts to convene arts leaders and develop a leadership learning community for them, they improved their relationships with each other, began working together, and now a few organizations are considering merging. So you set out to improve leadership capacity, but your leadership program had the unintended consequence of building collaboration among your grantees.

3. Evaluate to understand why.

Without an evaluation it isn't possible to understand exactly why your grant or initiative made an impact. Suppose you are funding youth development programs, and young people are now reporting less risky behavior than they had previously. If you don't evaluate it, you might not know whether that is because you worked to improve the quality of these youth development programs, or because a specific curriculum was introduced, or because the programs became more accessible to certain under-represented communities. Evaluation will help you to unpack and understand specifically what you did that made the difference.

4. Evaluate to inform future grantmaking.

One of the things that you can do when you evaluate (when you interview grantees or other stakeholders, for example) is find out how needs are changing. Evaluations are the time to ask questions like these: What's different about this issue now as compared to three years ago when you started your program? What might be needed in the future? What do you know now that you didn't know when the program began? The answers to these types of questions can help inform the next round of funding or highlight additional components that you might want to add to your grant program.

5. Evaluate to take responsibility.

Simply put, to be good stewards and to exercise your fiduciary responsibility, you need to have confidence that your grant dollars are used to make a positive impact. Spending time and resources to conduct evaluations will help your foundation continue to thrive and achieve results.

You might have a new-found sense of the importance of conducting evaluations, but that doesn't mean you have to evaluate every grant, initiative, or program. In fact, my final tip is this: Don't try to evaluate everything. Not only is it impossible, it isn't even beneficial. You probably don't have the resources to evaluate in all of those areas, and you should be focusing on what's most important to learn and where your evaluation resources are best deployed.

The reasons to conduct evaluations are compelling. Evaluations provide information to better understand consequences—intended and unintended—and to shine light on future grantmaking. These critical financial decisions should be made with insight and information, maximizing resources and, ultimately, impact. Good evaluations make all the difference.

● ● ●

OOPS, I FORGOT TO EVALUATE!

It's year five of your five-year funding initiative, and you need to report progress to your board and determine whether another round of funding is warranted. You're thinking, "Darn, I wish I had included evaluation planning when we developed this initiative. Now I'd have a better way to show our results."

Sound familiar? Don't worry; you aren't alone. Many funders don't think about evaluation at the outset (or they do think about it but choose to allocate resources completely on the program, rather than including assessment). There are three things you can do now—retrospectively—to learn from the past and inform your future. I recommend doing this with the help of an external evaluation consultant. He or she will be more objective, will be able to devote the time needed, and will be more likely to elicit honest feedback from grantees and stakeholders at a time when additional funding is at stake.

Fortunately, conducting a retrospective evaluation is as simple as look, listen, and learn.

1. **Look at reported accomplishments and compare them to objectives.** Your grantees identified their project goals and objectives in their proposals, and hopefully they reported on their progress in

their annual grant reports. You can review these documents to determine which objectives were met (or exceeded) and which weren't. Additionally, your grantees might have highlighted some unintended achieved outcomes that weren't part of the original plan. Those should be documented too, as well as barriers that prevented grantees from meeting all of their goals.

2. **Listen to your grantees.** Interview your grantees to learn what they see as major accomplishments, barriers, current needs, and opportunities for further investment. You could include the following questions among others you identify:

- Given your goals (or the goals of the initiative), where were you most successful?
- What do you think were your most important accomplishments during the grant period?
- Were there any additional accomplishments related to this goal that weren't anticipated?
- What were some of the challenges you encountered that made it difficult to meet your goals? (These might be internal challenges such as staff turnover, or external challenges such as changes to the economy or policy environment.)
- What are the most pressing needs you (or the population being served) are facing now?
- If additional funding is available, where should we focus our resources over the next two to three years?
- If we/you could do it all over again, what should we/you do differently? (I call this "the question guaranteed to save your foundation time and money," as it will likely pull out the critical missteps and missed opportunities that can be rectified in the next phase of grantmaking.)

3. Learn from other key stakeholders and experts.

Now is a great time not only to learn about the impact of your current program but also to plan ahead for the next round of investments. The world has changed in the two, five, or 10 years since you planned your funding initiative, and so have the needs of your constituents. Local, national, and international experts and thought leaders can help inform you about these changes and opportunities. So can stakeholders who have been involved in your efforts but who weren't grant recipients (e.g., other funders, government officials, schools, parents, consumers, etc.). Learn from them by reviewing recent literature or by conducting interviews, surveys, or focus groups.

Although including a project-wide evaluation plan from the start of your initiative is always the best approach, it's not too late to create some meaningful lessons and metrics when your project is well underway or even winding to a close. Most retrospective evaluations can be conducted and reported within a matter of weeks. (In fact, you could accomplish the first step in a single day!) With the results in hand, you'll be able to better inform your board about the impact your project has had and provide data that will help make sure the next round of funding is money well spent.

FORTUNATELY, CONDUCTING A RETROSPECTIVE EVALUATION IS AS SIMPLE AS LOOK, LISTEN, AND LEARN.

Leverage

● ● ●

SMALL STONE, BIG RIPPLE: TWELVE STRATEGIES FOR SPREADING YOUR SMALL GRANT FURTHER

Do you want to make a big splash with grant dollars, but you can only make a small gift? Not a problem! Some of the most effective change starts with a small grant. Follow a few simple strategies to create a ripple effect with a small gift. **Here are 12 ideas to help you make a big impact.**

1. **Educate yourself.** Who else is funding your issue? What's needed and what can you do? Devote a day to researching your topic, and identify relevant experts and foundation program officers. Call or email them to learn more.

2. **Invest in a great leader.** Identify leaders you believe in, then support them. For example, provide executive coaching or management training so they can build a more effective team.

3. **Invest in a great organization.** Identify a nonprofit that is creating social change and provide help. Your funds for strategic planning, a feasibility study, communications activities, or management information systems will be cherished more than you know.

4. **Focus your giving.** Choose a single issue, region, or affected population. Identify proven organizations in that area and support their most promising projects.

5. **Provide multi-year funding.** When you support an organization over several successive years, you ensure that the staff can spend more time on programs and less on fund-raising. Your gift also tells other potential funders that this organization is worth serious commitment.

6. **Leverage your resources.** Can you pool resources with other grantmakers who share your passion? Join existing funding collaboratives, giving circles, donor networks, or community foundations.

7. **Convene nonprofit leaders.** You can play a critical role by simply bringing people together. Provide a conference room, reimburse meal or travel expenses, or help plan the meeting agenda. If you can't host, cover

the costs for a nonprofit staffer who couldn't attend a conference otherwise.

8. **Fund an evaluation.** Nonprofits know they need a thorough evaluation of their programs, but they also often lack the time, resources, and expertise. Even a modest grant can help organizations determine their impact by conducting surveys, interviews, or focus groups.

9. **Fund policy change.** Local, state, and national policies can have far-reaching impact on people and communities. Support policy change by funding research on critical issues. Fund media advocacy, policy advocacy organizations, and advocacy training for grassroots leaders.

10. **Provide program-related investments.** A PRI is a good investment if a nonprofit can generate income to repay your gift. Or make a below-market or no-interest loan, or pledge your credit as security for an organization's bank loan.

11. **Fund globally.** Small grants go far when you send them across the world. For example, make a donation to a community that is rebuilding after a tragedy (such as the typhoon in the Philippines), or support a local foundation there.

12. **Offer challenge grants.** Jump-start an organization's development efforts by offering a matching grant. Challenge grants have helped organizations raise money that exceeds their goals, inspiring entire communities to get involved.

With each gift you make, no matter the size, you empower others, encouraging new partnerships and laying the groundwork for future accomplishments. Make a list of three ways to make big change with small grants. Then choose just one small grant within the next two months to start your own ripple in the pond.

●   ●   ●

SIX WAYS TO FIND FUNDING PARTNERS

One of the best ways to increase the impact of your grantmaking is to leverage the funding and expertise of other foundations or individuals by developing funding partnerships. The trouble, of course, is that it's not always easy to figure out who else might want to partner with you on your project. In my experience, there are six easy ways to identify possible funders to support you and your work. **We'll take a quick look at each:**

1. **Ask staff of your local Regional Association of Grantmakers.** These individuals are working day in and day out with various foundations in your region, and they are keenly aware of the different issues and projects that are currently active. They will probably have some great suggestions and can even make introductions for you.

2. **Explore funder networks.** There are many national and local networks of foundations that have banded together to learn from each other and improve their grantmaking on certain topics, such as aging, health, or a specific ethnic population. It is well worth your time to investigate these groups.

3. **Convene a funder presentation or webinar about the topic.** Educating other funders on the need that your project is addressing can help identify those who might be interested in supporting your work. For instance, there are probably many foundations that fund

human services or education, but if they knew about the work that you're doing regarding literacy rates in your community, they might be eager to get involved.

4. **Ask your grantees.** Trust me, your grantees are hustling to find funders to support their issues. They are likely very aware of other funders in your community, or even statewide or nationally, that might be interested in contributing to your work.

5. **Use funder databases.** These are wonderful tools that can help you find funders interested in your topic. Check out the Foundation Center, which has an online directory that you can use to identify other funders either in your community or nationally.

6. **Create a donor-advised fund at your local community foundation.** Funding partners don't have to be foundations; they can be individuals. You could set up a donor-advised fund to find support for your effort, and a community foundation can help you identify the people or families that may be interested in supporting it.

Could you benefit right now from leveraging other funders—their resources as well as their knowledge and expertise? I encourage you to explore these options to identify funding partners. The payoff will be well worth the effort.

● ● ●

SIX WAYS TO ENGAGE YOUR STAKEHOLDERS

Key stakeholders have much to contribute to the decision-making process, and their involvement can dramatically improve the success of any funding program. Here we'll examine six ways to leverage stakeholders and benefit from their input—but first let's discuss who those key stakeholders are.

There are three types of stakeholders:

- **The first** are those most directly impacted by the problem you are trying to solve, the ones feeling the pain of the issue. They could be families living in the local neighborhood, youth in the school system, or women who are surviving domestic violence.
- **The second group** is made up of the people who are attempting to solve the problem—whether they are neighborhood residents, nonprofit leaders, researchers, policy makers, or experts at any level.
- **The third category** includes those people who could be solving the problem with you, except that they either aren't fully aware of their role or they don't realize that the problem exists. For example, you might be trying to support youth employment in your community because you are concerned that many teens are not getting the job skills or training necessary to achieve success as young adults. The CEOs of banks or corporations within your community might not be aware of this problem—or feel any connection to it. But you can help them understand, for example, that the success of their community and their businesses depends on a thriving workforce. Then they may see the importance of partnering with you on this youth employment project in order to protect their own futures.

All three categories of stakeholders can be engaged and involved in decision making. All have valuable contributions to make to the success of your programs and initiatives. Let's take a brief look at six ways stakeholders can help you in our grantmaking.

1. **Understanding.** In the early stages of your grantmaking and program development, you could engage stakeholders to help you understand the issues. Ask them questions like these: What are some of the challenges you face? Where are the greatest challenges—in a certain part of your city, in a certain type of population, among particular kinds of organizations? Key stakeholders can help you think through and understand the issues, and the nuances of those issues.

2. **Weighing options.** Once you have some ideas as to the direction of your grantmaking, you can vet your ideas with key stakeholders to help you better consider the pros and cons of different approaches. For instance, suppose you want to address substance abuse, but you're not sure whether to focus on treatment or prevention. Speaking with key stakeholders can provide a chance to understand some of the challenges and opportunities within each of these areas. That input should reveal valuable information and real-world wisdom to help you make an informed choice. It should also provide a heads-up regarding potential pitfalls.

3. **Prioritizing.** Once you've developed the five or six areas that you think you could successfully focus on, you can engage key stakeholders to help you prioritize among those areas. What's the most burning issue? Where could you have an early impact? What is some of the low-hanging fruit that could allow for immediate success? And what are some of the more challenging topics that you want to address down the road, once your efforts are underway? Feedback in this early stage is critical and can have a major impact on success rates.

4. **Implementing.** Stakeholders can become key partners in helping you with implementation. It might be the nonprofit organization that you fund to launch a new

intervention related to domestic violence, for example. It could be the university, and the researchers at that university, whom you engage to collect data and help inform the progress of your approach. It could be a policy maker who helps you scale your efforts to a statewide or even national level. It is better to work together than alone. Develop partnerships with your stakeholders as you implement your ideas.

5. Cheerleading. Stakeholders can become champions. If you have engaged them from the beginning and kept them abreast of your progress and decision making, then they'll buy in to what you are trying to accomplish. Get that buy-in, and they may help spread the word about what you are trying to achieve. This, in turn, can engage other stakeholders and leverage additional resources to support your work.

6. Evaluating. Stakeholders can be involved in evaluation planning, and they can inform your evaluation team about what's working and what's not working from their perspectives. Whether these stakeholders are grantees or outside observers, they'll probably have a lot to say. Based on their feedback and other evaluation findings, you can take the cycle back to the beginning and engage those stakeholders in additional planning, refining, and refocusing of your grantmaking program.

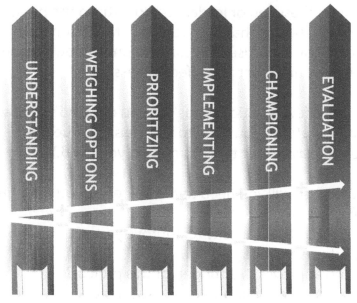

INCREASED VALUE OF STAKEHOLDER ENGAGEMENT

UNDERSTANDING · WEIGHING OPTIONS · PRIORITIZING · IMPLEMENTING · CHAMPIONING · EVALUATION

It is to everyone's advantage to involve stakeholders in decision making. Their feedback and involvement can make a tremendous difference in success versus failure for any initiative. Ask yourself: Who are your stakeholders? How are you engaging them? What can you do right now to reach out to those you've overlooked? Get your stakeholders involved. Working together to address issues is the best way to make progress.

• • •

WHO'S IN CHARGE?

In an age of partnerships, collaboration, and leverage, we are increasingly reliant on other organizations and partners to play vital roles in our work. But we partner with people, not organizations. It's important to take a moment consider who we are partnering with within the organization, whether they are the right people, and who else must be engaged.

It is critical that top decision makers, often the CEO and board chair, fully understand and support the project and are involved at some level. After all, if things start to go south, these senior leaders could jettison the project before you have a chance to rescue it. More significantly, their insight, expertise, and connections can be leveraged advance your impact and effectiveness.

Here are a few questions to ask to find out who's in **charge.** (Hint: Sometimes you need to ask the same question a few different ways to get the information you need.)

- Who else will you need to talk to before you can agree to participate?
- Who has the authority to approve your organization's partnership today?
- Who approves the budget for this project?
- If your organization were to issue a press release about its involvement in this project, who would be quoted?
- You want to talk to these leaders and understand from their perspective—and from their lips—the value they see in this project, as well as their concerns or hesitations. This is best done in person, where you can also observe their body language. You do not want to rely on someone else (e.g., a program officer or project manager) to interpret this for you, as they might downplay concerns.

Armed with this insight, you can make sure the project provides this value to this partner. You can also directly address the concerns during the conversation and in an ongoing manner ("Yes, we are also concerned that the success of this effort long term depends on the bond levy passing. However, polling indicates likelihood of passage and we have a Plan B in case it doesn't. I will personally keep you apprised of this periodically over the next six months.").

You can also use this opportunity to suggest ways that senior leaders who aren't involved in the day-to-day work can stay informed and engaged in a way that is convenient and meaningful to them. **For example, this might be:**

- Monthly or quarterly CEO breakfast briefing
- Periodic email updates
- Regularly scheduled 20-minute phone conversations
- Participation in key events
- Speaking opportunities
- Involving this leader in making introductions to other key leaders
- Special access to thought leaders and decision makers engaged in this project (e.g., special reception with a nationally known speaker; roundtable discussion with state legislators)

Knowing who is in charge for each of the partners you work with can save hours and hours of wasted time and countless amounts of frustration. By addressing the concerns of key leaders and securing their buy-in from the start, you'll secure more impact for the work you do together.

ONE OF THE BEST WAYS TO INCREASE THE IMPACT OF YOUR GRANTMAKING IS TO LEVERAGE THE FUNDING AND EXPERTISE OF OTHER FOUNDATIONS AND INDIVIDUALS BY DEVELOPING FUNDING PARTNERSHIPS.

Philanthropic
Mindset

FOUR STEPPARENTING LESSONS FOR GRANTMAKERS

I'm a stepparent and a stepchild. Apparently I am not alone. A staggering 42 percent of U.S. adults have a step-relationship—either a stepparent, a step- or half-sibling, or a stepchild. This translates to 95.5 million adults and doesn't include all the step-kids under 18. This number is actually larger, when you count all the boyfriends, girlfriends, and fiancés of people with step-kids, plus those kids themselves. Essentially, there's a whole bunch of adults and children wondering, "Who is this person, why are they in my life, and what am I supposed to do with them?"

Here are four stepparenting lessons I've learned that apply to philanthropy and consulting:

1. **You have all the responsibility and zero authority.** As a stepparent, you might be packing your step-kids' lunches and getting them to school on time, but you have no legal authority. You aren't their parent, so you don't get to make major decisions. But you can have an impact. Early on I realized that while I would never be the first person my step-kids would turn to for emotional support, I could help get them into college. Thirty campus visits, multiple rounds of ACT tutoring, and countless reminders of application deadlines later, my oldest stepchild has graduated college, another is a college senior, and a third is enrolled in community college.

   Similarly, grantmakers are responsible for the outcomes of their funding initiative, yet they have no real authority to realize those results. Outcomes depend on the success of grantees, the willingness of partners to collaborate, changing political environments, and the economy. But your chances of success are greater if you pick one thing you can impact and align your resources toward that goal.

2. **You didn't build this road and you aren't driving the bus.** Stepparenting is like hopping into a moving car. There you are with your step-kids, your spouse, and his or her ex. You didn't plan this road trip, you don't get to choose the destination, and no one is handing you the wheel. The best you can do is pull out a map and offer suggestions.

   Similarly, professional grantmakers did not invent the social problems they are trying to fix, nor have most guided the foundation since its inception. But you can influence the outcome. Well-informed, data-driven strategies and best practices can be your road map to increase your chances of impact.

3. **People will appreciate you . . . 20 years from now.** If you are hoping your young or teenage step-kids will remember you on Mother's/Father's Day or submit your name for the parent-of-the-year award, think again. You definitely aren't in this for the glory. Your moral compass is what guides you to do the best that you can for these children. Stick with it, be consistent, and tell them you love them no matter what. One day when they are in college or raising their own kids they will tell you how much they appreciate you, and you will see the fruits of your labor in how well they turned out.

   Similarly, as grantmakers we often don't get applauded for the ultimate impact of our grantmaking strategies. We fund early childhood programs but rarely get to see when those preschoolers graduate high school or college. But, no matter what, we keep our eyes on the prize.

4. **You aren't alone.** Early in my stepparenting life I desperately searched for other stepmoms, preferably those with step-teenagers but also small children of their own, like me. I haven't met many, but when I do we bond instantly and make immediate plans to share experiences and compare notes—preferably over cocktails.

   Similarly, working in philanthropy can be lonely, especially if you are new. However, there are resources to turn to for ideas and support. Join Emerging Practitioners in Philanthropy, participate in your local regional association of grantmakers, or see if there is an affinity group in your program area. If you are a consultant, join the National Network of Consultants to Grantmakers.

You didn't start the situation and you don't have all the knowledge and resources you need to solve it. But if you trust your instincts, get the advice and support you need, and stay the course, you will be 80 percent ahead of the game—and you will make a difference!

● ● ●

WHAT BEING PREGNANT WITH TWINS TAUGHT ME ABOUT PHILANTHROPY

Almost every aspiring mom (and dad) has big plans and preconceived ideas about what pregnancy will be like. You picture the way your life might change, you plan out a nursery, order a crib—it's pretty straightforward stuff. Straightforward, that is, until you discover you're having twins. Suddenly, all those plans and preconceptions go out the window, and you have to rethink everything. The basic premise is still the same—you're bringing new life into the world and want to raise it well—but now the reality in which you'll operate is vastly different than expected.

The realities in which foundations operate bring similar shifts and challenges on a regular basis. We start out our careers or our new initiatives with clear hopes and goals for the good we will accomplish, only to find that real life has other plans. Frequently, we must learn lessons of humility and adaptability, and rethink what was already well thought out.

Fortunately, there are four lessons from twin pregnancy that I've learned to apply to philanthropy:

1. **Always accept offers of help.** On a plane, if someone offers to help put your luggage in the overhead compartment, always say yes. When they walk around offering you water, always say yes. Want to sit down? Yes. Want me to do the dishes? Yes. How about if I drive? Yes. Need advice on parenting twins? Yes. Want to take a nap? Yes!

One of the things I most enjoy and appreciate about philanthropy is that we have a culture of helping one another. Unlike Pepsi versus Coke, the Robert Wood Johnson Foundation doesn't need to worry that the Bill and Melinda Gates Foundation has planted spies among its employees, looking to steal the best new innovation in evaluation or access to health care. Generally speaking, we all want to help each other and advance the collective good. This means that at any given time there are many people, ideas, programs, conferences, training programs, coaches, and so on, ready and available to help you with whatever your need. Starting a new foundation? You can turn to your local regional association of grantmakers, Exponent Philanthropy, National Center on Family Philanthropy, the Council on Foundations, or a consultant for advice. New CEO? There are many programs and resources that want to help you. Developing a new grant program? There is probably an affinity group of funders who can offer ideas. And if you reach out to key leaders in your field, chances are high they will gladly schedule time to talk with you. Take advantage of this willingness to help—you will avoid pitfalls and achieve greater impact down the road.

2. **Reduce your expectations.** This might sound as if it flies in the face of my other advice about having an abundance mentality versus a poverty mentality, but hear me out.

When I was pregnant, I read an article that advised pregnant moms of multiples to immediately start reducing our expectations. It told us to make a list of everything we have on our plates—volunteer activities, household chores, work, classes, hobbies, entertaining, exercise, birthday party planning, grocery shopping, carpooling, public speaking, work-related travel, whatever. Then start crossing things off or ratcheting them down, because you simply won't be able to do it all and be a mom to two (or three or four) newborns. If you serve on a board of directors, take a leave for six months; tell the teacher you will no longer be available to volunteer in class this year; take the semester off your evening MBA program; ask neighbors to organize bringing you meals for the first month; tell colleagues you are no longer traveling more than 50 miles but would be happy to Skype. Instead, focus on maintaining the activities that are most helpful to your current situation and will give you energy. While I took time off of serving on my local community foundation board, I joined the local "moms of twins" club.

As funders, of course we should set high expectations for our organizations, our staff, and our grantees. But we should also be aware that we could easily work 72 hours days trying to get it all done, burn out our employees, and set up our grantees for failure and our boards for disappointment with unrealistic expectations. It is far better to prioritize the activities that provide the greatest impact, are the best use of our talents and assets, have the highest chance of success, and let the rest go for now. This isn't to say you won't invest enthusiastically in your goals, but instead of launching your five-pronged strategy to increase youth employment, make it two-pronged and phase the other three in later after the first two have early wins.

3. Get your infrastructure in place. A few months after my twins were born, my friend Rose asked how I was doing. "You know," I said, "It's not as hard as everyone makes it out to be." "That's because you have all your infrastructure in place," she replied. She was right. I made sure we bought a house that was flexible enough for new kids, three step-kids, a home office, and a guest room. I made sure we moved into a family-friendly neighborhood. I hired a nanny who started work two days after we brought the twins home from the hospital, so that I could continue to expand my consulting practice. We had a housecleaner. We lived near lots of family who could help us and we had a guest room where they could stay for a while. I married a man who gladly changed diapers and cooked dinner. I had my infrastructure in place to ease my transition into motherhood, and it helped me be a less stressed-out mom.

Grantmakers similarly need to make sure they have their infrastructure in place to position their staff and grantees for success, now and into the future. This can include ensuring adequate staff capacity, attending to leadership development across the organization, upgrading technology to allow staff to be productive while traveling, having a strategic communications plan to leverage the impact of your grants, hiring consultants to bring specific expertise, providing professional development opportunities for staff, providing technical assistance for grantees, regularly conducting evaluations so you know when and how to make course corrections, etc. A solid infrastructure not only can help reduce staff stress but also can better position your organization to adapt when those unexpected shifts occur.

4. **You can't obsess over everything.** While other pregnant moms of multiples were busy finding recipes for homemade baby food and cleaning their air ducts (because God forbid their babies might breath a dust molecule), I was helping my oldest stepdaughter apply to college, including organizing visits to many campuses (waddling around with my large belly). But while other moms of 17-year-olds were busy researching every college in depth and spending $50,000 (not kidding) on

tutors and college application coaches to help get their kids into the best university, I was busy thowing up.

The benefit of being pregnant while helping my stepdaughter get into college was that I didn't have time to obsess over either activity. I sort of got the twins' nursery ready, but it was not one that would be featured in a Pottery Barn Kids catalog. I encouraged and reminded my stepdaughter to apply early for the greatest chance of acceptance, but I didn't fill out the application for her to make it happen. I had to focus on the most essential, or what I was best suited to influence, and let the rest go.

In philanthropy, there are endless societal problems to tackle and many high-performing leaders, innovations, and solutions to support. We simply can't do it all, or do it all well. We are better off focusing on fewer causes, fewer strategies, a more limited geographic area, or some other way to narrow and prioritize our work. Ask yourself, "If our foundation could only accomplish one thing with this funding initiative over the next three years, what should it be? Realistically, what can it be?" Focus on that first. As you get going you might choose to expand, or you might choose to go deeper.

Philanthropy, like life, is always full of surprises that require reconsideration and adjustment—and that's a good thing. If things are always completely controlled and predictable, then what's the point? Being able to learn and adjust as you go—both about your work and yourself—is a gift. It not only keeps you sane but frequently opens the door to an opportunity or reward that you never could have envisioned. And that is what keeps our work exciting, engaging, and worthwhile.

YOUR CHANCES OF SUCCESS ARE GREATER IF YOU PICK ONE THING YOU CAN IMPACT AND ALIGN YOUR RESOURCES TOWARD THAT GOAL.

Self-Improvement

PURGE, PLAN, REWARD: YOUR THREE-STEP PROCESS FOR GETTING ANYTHING DONE QUICKLY

For once I would like to enter autumn feeling on top of things: my client work mapped out for the year, a clear understanding of how to meet my remaining annual goals in these next four months, and my kids' school activities listed in my calendar. I would like to look fabulous in a wardrobe of "fall transitional clothes" rather than resemble Eric Carle's Mixed-up Chameleon in some crazy combo of flip-flops, cotton dresses, and wool sweaters.

So I've decided to implement a three-step process to solve my fall dilemma: Purge, Plan, Reward. **I'm going to block out three solid days in the next month to:**

Purge:

Out with the old (or the stressful, or the irrelevant) before starting something new. My mile-long to-do list stresses me out and prevents me from setting my top three priorities. So I'm going to delete it. If it hasn't been done in six months, it probably isn't that important. I'm also going to clean out my office and throw out anything that makes me think guiltily, "Oh, I really should [fill in the blank]": industry reports from last year I've been meaning to read, files of prospective clients too busy to meet with me, etc. I need to start fresh.

Plan:

Make a plan, make sure it is realistic, and carve out time to accomplish it. I will (1) list all my current and pipeline projects from now through December, (2) review this year's goals to see what I still need to do and add what is realistic to that list, (3) identify all remaining travel and plan for it (transportation arrangements, child care, budgeting, etc.). Note that I am not adding every single thing I would like to accomplish in life into this three-month plan!

Reward:

After all that purging and planning, we need to treat ourselves. Notice that the rewarding comes before the implementing. What will I do? Go shopping, of course! Hey, even moms need new back-to-school clothes. I'm taking myself out for a day— yes, a whole day by myself, without kids.

You can apply this process to quickly solve any problem in your personal or professional life. Here are some examples:

1. **You want to get married and your boyfriend of two years isn't sure he wants to commit?**

   - **Purge:** Break up with him, gather up all his things in a box, and mail it to him.
   - **Plan:** Make a list of 50 positive qualities you want in a relationship (like monogamy), sign up for a couple

of online dating services, and only date people who meet your most important qualities.

- **Reward:** A girls' getaway weekend, a massage, a long hike—whatever makes you feel good.

2. You need to plan and launch a new grantmaking initiative?

- **Purge:** Spend a couple of hours jotting down possibilities: possible goals, strategies, grantees, consultants. Now purge. Literally cross out everything that you think is unrealistic, unsuccessful, annoying, or stressful even to think about. Goals that will take you off course? Delete. Strategies that are the same worn-out, time-consuming approaches? Cross out. Grantees that are good on paper but never seem to deliver? Remove. Consultants whom everyone recommends but you don't like? Oust. Another purge: What current work can you delegate to someone else so you have time to design this initiative?
- **Plan:** Now sit down and write up a six-month plan to develop the initiative, based on your remaining possible goals, strategies, grantees, and consultants. Add in things like determining existing resources you can build upon, identifying data sources, and identifying potential funding sources.
- **Reward:** Now that you have a plan in place, take a day off. Do something fun: Spend the day with your kids, go to a museum, explore a new neighborhood. You will return refreshed and ready to implement your plan.

So think about it. What is something you need to get done quickly? What should be purged to physically or mentally clear out space so that you can accomplish it? What are the three, five, or 10 steps that you need to take to get it done? What is a nice carrot at the end of this short stick that would make you feel happy? Go do it!

EVERYTHING I NEED TO KNOW I ALREADY KNEW, BUT FORGOT

My business coach, Alan Weiss, frequently writes, "I can't believe how stupid I was two weeks ago," meaning that he just learned something new and he can't believe he didn't realize it before. I get it. We all need to continuously learn new things and improve. But I am constantly surprised by what I used to know, then somehow completely forgot, then had to relearn all over again—only then to remember that I used to know it.

This happens to me all the time. For example: I'm sitting in my backyard writing a proposal for a new project that I am extremely excited about. It's about three weeks overdue. I'm asking myself why I've been so busy that I haven't had three solid hours in three weeks to write it. My mind flits around to the meetings, deadlines, events, reports, and sleepless nights of the past weeks—time spent chained to my computer and dedicated to my clients, at the expense of my children, husband, and future revenue.

And then I remember.

A previous business coach once explained to me that if I want to be the CEO of my consulting practice (as opposed to the owner-operator), then my own time should represent no more than 10 percent of the total project engagement. That's maybe a handful of hours per week. My projects should be staffed and managed by the very excellent and talented consultants I regularly identify, cultivate, and train. I need the rest of the time for business development, writing, and being available to deal with any problems or crises.

I followed his advice and it worked! I worked less, I accomplished more, and my business grew. My clients continued to be delighted with the value we provided. But somehow I slid backward. I mindlessly eased back into old habits. I forgot. Maybe it was the recession, when clients were harder to come by and I had more time of my own to dedicate to them. Maybe it was "baby brain" (I had twins, does that mean I lost twice as much brain power?). And, OK, my father and the mother of my subcontractor on this potential project both had extreme, unexpected health problems during one two-week period (both recovered). But life happens. What worked for me in 2005 should certainly work for me now. And I should have retained this practice over the years, not forgotten about it.

So here is what I am going to do about it (this should be easy, since I've done this all before):

- Immediately identify current projects that could benefit from additional talent on the Putnam team. Identify and retain that talent. Dedicate my time to bringing them up to speed and positioning them for success.
- When talking with a prospective client, if I think it is at all likely that it will result in a new project, I will immediately begin to identify my staffing plan and other consultants I can bring onto our team (rather than waiting until the proposal is approved).
- "Audit" myself. Regularly review how I allocated my time at the beginning of a project and how my time was actually spent by the conclusion. Look for themes. What were the factors that led to success? What were the factors that caused me to delve in too deep? How can I improve?
- Write this up and put it on my office wall. I'm a visual learner. I have less chance of forgetting something important if it is written in large letters in a place I frequently look.

So I ask you: What did you know and do two years ago that you have completely forgotten about? This could be big (you decided to pursue a leadership position at a larger foundation, but you find yourself in the same old role today), modest (you started meeting regularly with your direct reports to help them troubleshoot problems, but everyone got busy and you stopped doing it), or small but important (you committed to responding to grantseeker inquiries within 48 hours and clearing out your inbox weekly, but you have 569 unread emails).

What are one to two things you can do differently right now? What are another one to two things you can do differently going forward? Do them. Trust me, three years from now you will be glad that you did.

● ● ●

STEP OVER INERT BODIES

"It takes a while before you can step over inert bodies and go ahead with what you were trying to do."

I first read this quote from artist Jenny Holzer while visiting the Minneapolis Sculpture Garden. I think it offers profound advice for us, both in life and professionally as grantmakers. **How often have you:**

- Dated someone who never quite got around to making something of life (getting a job, seeking promotion, finishing graduate school, etc.)?
- Had a friend who never seemed happy when your life was going well (new job, birth of a child), because she was never happy with hers?
- Wondered why a parent told you how much she loved you, but her actions never felt loving?

Similarly, as a grantmaker, how often have you:

- Funded a nonprofit leader who had a great reputation but never really delivered as promised?
- Tried to partner with another funder who put up roadblocks every step of the way?

124

- Sought to introduce a new best practice into an existing grant program, only to be told, "Don't rock the boat"?
- Been encouraged by your board chair to evaluate your impact but then been discouraged from making any real change?

They are inert bodies. Step over them.

We need to recognize when people in our personal or professional lives are inert. When they don't want to change, grow, advance, or improve. And then we need to literally move past them toward the future we envision for ourselves and our communities. Break up with the girlfriend, make new friends, fund leaders whose impact is groundbreaking, connect with colleagues who share your vision, seek a new position with a forward-thinking organization, and find new board members.

STEPPING OVER INERT BODIES

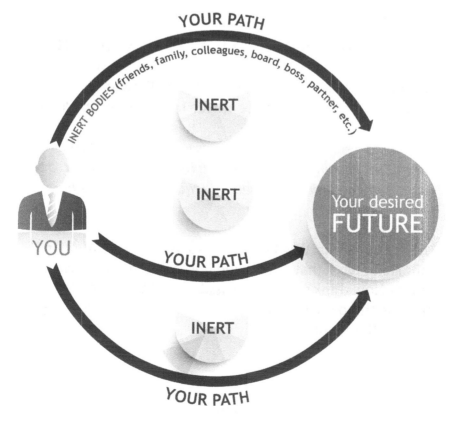

Here are four ways to recognize when a person in your personal or professional life is inert:

- You are asking the same questions over and over again, to the point where you anticipate the answer.
- You feel energized with new ideas and opportunities, but when you share those ideas with this person, you feel drained and deflated.
- You wonder why something promised never became a reality. Again.
- Your efforts to improve your foundation's grantmaking strategies, through best practices, new technologies, and efficient operations, fall on deaf ears.

If you anticipate that no matter what you try, do, or say, nothing will change, that's great! It means you can say to yourself, "Oh, right, this person is inert!" and go around them.

● ● ●

DON'T ACT AGAINST YOUR NATURE

Another of my favorite quotes from the Minneapolis Sculpture Garden offers sage advice for philanthropy leaders:

You should limit the number of times you act against your nature, like sleeping with people you hate. It's interesting to test your capabilities for a while, but too much will cause damage.
— Jenny Holzer

Think about this: What is one thing you are tolerating in your life or work that makes you miserable, angry, frustrated, or sad? Now think for a moment about all the damage that one thing is causing you, along with your colleagues, organizations, and families.

Here are some examples of foundation leaders I know who failed to trust their instincts and went against their natures—and the problems it caused:

- A senior leader of a private foundation made a grant to an organization even though instinctively she didn't trust the leader. She did it because the organization was the right fit for an initiative she was involved in and she felt pressured to make the grant quickly. Her instinct was proven correct when this leader poorly represented the foundation and himself in public meetings.
- A family foundation CEO allowed his donor trustee to be inappropriately involved in micromanaging certain activities of the foundation, causing significant stress and frustration among the employees who had to spend countless hours placating the trustee and living with his mistakes.
- A health foundation program director ignored her instinct about hiring a consultant. She liked the firm's principals, but not the consultant they assigned to her project. Significant time and money were lost when the consultant failed to understand the foundation's needs and couldn't deliver.
- A foundation CEO stated for months that a certain employee needed to be fired due to poor performance but felt bad about firing him and kept putting it off. In the meantime, other employees were frustrated that the CEO tolerated the behavior, and it caused them to have doubts about the CEO's leadership and judgment.

In each of these cases, the foundation leader knew instinctively and immediately what to do. But they "acted against their nature" and failed to trust their instincts. The result was damage to personal and organizational reputations, misspent funds, loss of time, and frustrated staff. Just because you can tolerate bad behavior and poor performance, it doesn't mean you should.

So think back on the example you thought of earlier, the one thing you are tolerating that makes you miserable, angry, frustrated, or sad. You know what to do about it. Make a change.

HOW CAN YOU STAND OUT FROM THE CROWD?

Dropping my twins off at preschool one day, I slowed down (along with all the other cars on a six-lane road) to watch a small gaggle of geese walk slowly across. After explaining (unsuccessfully) to my kids that the plural of "goose" is "geese," not "gooses," we talked about how interesting it was that the geese chose to walk across the street when they could have flown.

What made us all stop and pay attention was that the geese did something unusual, something unexpected. They walked. They did this at some risk to themselves (they could have been hit by a car), but they didn't seem to care.

I've chosen to stand out from the crowd of other philanthropy consultants by sharing my own knowledge about philanthropy and grantmaking extensively and freely via articles, podcasts, blogs, and a weekly newsletter, rather than hiding behind the external validation of extensive research and client-approved reports. While I'm not likely to be hit by a car, this did involve a bit of risk taking on my part ("What if it's not well received?" "What if funders disagree with what I have to say?"). But standing out from the crowd means doing something new. It means knowing what you are already fully capable of (flying) and trying an alternative (walking). People will pay attention. And if you are adding value, they will appreciate it.

Ask yourself:

- What can I do this year to stand out from the crowd?
- What is the "same old, same old" I'm currently doing? How can I take it up a notch (or two)?

- What fear is holding me back?
- How will I feel five to 10 years from now if I don't make these changes?

All of us have some way to stand out, even if we don't recognize it right away. What's your standout opportunity, and how will you take advantage of it?

STANDING OUT FROM THE CROWD MEANS DOING SOMETHING NEW. IT MEANS KNOWING WHAT YOU ARE ALREADY FULLY CAPABLE OF, AND TRYING AN ALTERNATIVE. PEOPLE WILL PAY ATTENTION. AND IF YOU ARE ADDING VALUE, THEY WILL APPRECIATE IT.

• • •

Working with Consultants

TWENTY WAYS A CONSULTANT CAN MAKE YOUR LIFE EASIER

You and your staff can probably, collectively, leap tall buildings in a single bound. But you might not be able—or willing—to tackle every single need that presents itself to your organization. It might be time to hire a consultant. You only have so much time, and sometimes you need a new perspective and a helping hand from someone with an unbiased view and different expertise. If you are wondering just how much help consultants can be, here are 20 ways they can make your life easier.

1. **Perform needs assessments.** The more ingrained we get in our work, the harder it is to see the big picture of our organization's real needs. We may think we need a new grantmaking strategy or an update of our vision, but do we really? A strategic consultant can provide you with an overview of your organization and your work and help you determine where you have real gaps and where you need to make strategic change.

2. **Conduct environmental scans.** It would be great to know who else is doing similar work to yours, so you can best complement one another rather than unwittingly compete. And we would all like to know what major new developments are afoot in our field. But you simply don't have time to do the research necessary. A research consultant may be the best resource for you to learn more about who is doing what work, what's working, and what changes are on the horizon.

3. **Research grantmaking strategies.** If you are in the habit of making grants the same way you have for years, it might just be time to take a look at some new grantmaking strategies. Do you need to rethink your mission? The types of grants you make? The grant size? Or the region in which you make grants? All these questions can be overwhelming. Hiring a consultant to help you research and rethink the best ways to use your funds can help you see financial and organizational benefits now and in the future.

4. **Advise on program development.** A consultant with a particular area of expertise—education, grassroots advocacy, mental health, etc.—may provide you with the support you need as you create and grow your foundation's programs. You are the expert on your foundation, your community, your strategy. Let a consultant be the expert on the program details. This will help you build a better program, and having an expert's knowledge and support will help you raise your foundation's status as a go-to resource for that topic.

5. **Review proposals.** When you put out a request for proposals, you get proposals back. Do you really have the time to read and carefully consider each one? Strategic grantmaking requires more than just a scan of proposals. Hiring one or two consultants to read proposals and provide you with the strongest candidates can save you time and ensure you are making the best decisions for your grantmaking dollars.

6. Conduct site visits. Conducting site visits helps build relationships and ensure that your grantmaking dollars are going to the grantees who will put them to the best use. Unfortunately, scheduling conflicts and lack of time often get in the way of a good site visit. Hiring someone to organize and conduct site visits ensures that potential and current grantees are given the time and attention they deserve; in return, you receive an unbiased report of the site visit results. This is a win for everyone involved.

7. Coordinate the entire review process. For larger grantmaking programs, managing the flow of hundreds of applications and narrowing them down to finalists can be overwhelming. A consultant can help you orchestrate a system for review, including gathering and coordinating individual reviewers, answering applicant questions, and coordinating site visits among finalists. That means you can concentrate on overall supervision and review only the most promising applications.

8. Help with organizational development. Board development, staff development, administrative needs, technical support. Where do you begin when it comes to organizational development for your foundation? An expert can help you build your board strategically, provide staff training where necessary, and offer technical support and administrative cost-cutting techniques. By bringing in an efficiency expert, or several experts with different skills, you will see stronger short-term and long-term changes within your organization.

9. **Explore ideas for new foundations.** Are you considering creating a new foundation? Do you have an idea for integrated health care, academic changes, or social justice programs for which you see funding gaps? Before you contact an attorney to get started on creating your new foundation, bring someone on board to see what the real needs are, where someone else might be doing similar work, and what changes need to be made to current funding and programs. An investment on the front end will save you time and legal fees down the road.

10. **Assist with ongoing management.** Do you need help with day-to-day tasks that have become overwhelming because of unforeseen circumstances or because you have hit the "busy season"? Bringing someone in temporarily to help review proposals or respond to applicant questions, or to help you get reorganized, is a great use of financial resources. Your investment in project support ensures a seamless and professionally run organization.

11. **Facilitate board and staff retreats.** A half-day, full-day, or multi-day retreat is challenging at best. Covering fund-raising, grantmaking strategy, general operational business, and more requires an outsider. A retreat facilitator will create an agenda that ensures that you are covering the right topics, keep participants on track and out of "rabbit holes," listen for common themes and concerns, and, in the end, help you create and implement a strategy for the future. A great facilitator is one person you always want to consider for your team.

12. **Negotiate multi-generational dynamics for family philanthropies.** When you run a family philanthropy, there is no way around family dynamics getting into the mix. Unlike other businesses and philanthropies, at the end of the day, you don't get to walk away from the relationship challenges of a family endeavor. Keep the personal conflicts out of your business and homes by hiring a consultant to help negotiate the communication efforts and philanthropic challenges that arise when your family's generations and personalities conflict.

13. Guide succession planning. Both family philanthropies and other foundations face inevitable changes in leadership. The key is to be well prepared before transition occurs and to plan for it carefully, sensitively, and professionally. Hiring a consultant who specializes in succession planning will help you avoid interpersonal conflict and give everyone a clear, common vision of how your foundation's leadership will evolve.

14. Help with leadership development and coaching. When you are responsible for making big decisions, you are perceived as a leader in your organization, in your community, and in your field. Make sure that your words and actions match your leadership role. A good leadership coach will help you outline your goals and ensure that you are able to communicate clearly and effectively, garner support from other leaders, and galvanize others to build community and make change.

15. Conduct executive searches. When you are ready to hire an executive staff member, the legwork involved in getting to the right executives and screening individuals is challenging. Aside from the time involved, you may be looking at a pool of executives with whom you already have relationships and who need to ensure that discretion is a priority in discussions. Working with an executive search firm to handle initial discussions may be a great option for executive-level hiring.

16. Perform evaluations. When you are close to your grantmaking work and care passionately about it, it can be difficult to be objective. Yet scientific and objective evaluations may be key to sustaining investment in your program over the long term. An outside evaluation consultant can provide a clear, unbiased picture of your program's effectiveness and help you recognize successes, anticipate upcoming challenges, and make plans for improvement that will enhance sustainability. On the flip side, a good evaluation can also show that other investments may be more fruitful for your foundation.

17. Develop marketing communications. Communication and marketing strategy require communication and marketing experts. Often we think we can create a communications plan for an initiative, handle media relations, develop a budget, and create a compelling visual campaign. What we end up with is a weak effort made weaker by our lack of time and expertise, and finances that are squandered. A good communications consultant is going to save you time and, ultimately, provide you with a financial savings.

18. Strengthen your brand. Whether you know it or not, your foundation has a brand and an image. An expert branding consultant will help you decide what the brand will be and how it will be projected, rather than allowing uncoordinated internal actions or outside forces to shape your image. Once you have developed a clear brand and brand strategy, you'll find it enhances every aspect of your programmatic and communications work.

19. Provide legal or financial advice. Some situations simply require a consultant, no questions asked. When you need financial advice or legal expertise, you need a finance professional or an attorney. With all of the loopholes and unknowns in these areas, you never want to risk taking a chance or making a mistake that can be financially draining or devastating to your organization's reputation. Hire an attorney or financial advisor/CPA with expertise in philanthropy and the nonprofit sector.

20. **Explore new funding.** Does your foundation need new resources for funding options? Have you tapped your usual businesses, community partners, and donors? Where can you find new financial resources? There are people who are devoted to finding you new revenue streams. They already have ideas that you haven't considered, and they can research more. Let them partner with you to learn your needs and share what is out there with you. They may even be able to make introductions for you to make the first meeting a little easier.

Consultants can assist your foundation or nonprofit in just about any aspect of your work. Bringing one on board may be the best decision you make today. Think about where you might need some new views or a person who can devote more time to a project. And then do some research about consultants who have what you need. Explore the list of vetted consultants at the National Network of Consultants to Grantmakers (http://nncg.org) and ask other foundations or trusted partners about whom they used. By developing a list of potential consultants now, you will save yourself valuable time when you need one in the future.

● ● ●

WHY RFPS WASTE TIME: CHOOSE A BETTER APPROACH TO FINDING A GREAT CONSULTANT

Chances are, you've been in this position: The foundation for which you work needs to find consulting expertise to help with a particular project, program, initiative, etc. Everyone agrees that the first step is to develop an RFP so you can get qualified consultants to respond. It's a thorough, fair, and transparent process. Right?

Wrong.

I rarely respond to RFPs for consulting engagements. Their expectations are often unrealistic or undefined (not thorough), I rarely have an opportunity to discuss the project goals with decision makers (not fair), and I have no idea who or how many consultants I am competing against (not transparent). Because of this, I find RFPs to be, on the whole, not a good use of time and a considerable impediment to my ability to improve our clients' conditions.

What's worse, many foundations fail to understand how creating an RFP process for finding consultants can be a waste of their own time and an impediment to securing the best services and best value.

Foundations use RFPs to find consultants for four primary reasons:

1. They hope the consultants' proposals provide them with free insights into how best to implement the project (which they will then use without compensating the consultant).

2. They aren't aware of many consultants and they hope the RFP process identifies quality consultants.

3. They believe the RFP process demonstrates the holy grail of "transparency."

4. They declare it to be "our policy."

All of these reasons are flawed. While there is nothing wrong with seeking free advice, identifying quality consultants, wanting to ensure transparency, or creating standard policies for hiring consultants, none of these goals requires the use of a time-consuming and talent-limiting RFP process. **Here's why RFPs rarely fulfill their goals, as well as a look at some better alternatives:**

1. **Using RFPs to get free advice.** I once had a client at a family foundation solicit consultants using an RFP, and he specifically told me that his plan was to identify the best ideas from all the proposals and then have the chosen consultant (likely the cheapest) implement them. Like most consultants, I find this approach completely offensive. It takes a tremendous amount of unpaid time and uncompensated resources for a consultant to put together a well-considered scope of work, budget, and proposal. And every proposal is infused with the proprietary intellect, creativity, and experience of the consultant. It is not the job of consultants—often sole proprietors without consistent income—to subsidize philanthropic foundations that have millions or billions in assets. If a grantmaker is not aware of the best approaches to tackling a project, then it should either pay for that information or it should solicit it in honest, risk-free ways.

   What's better: I would much rather meet a foundation president for lunch and share free advice about ways they could plan a project than spend 16 hours putting together a proposal that might or might not get approved. In fact, I'd rather give an hour of free advice for a project I know I won't get than spend hours working on an RFP response for a project I might get. It's a much more honest relationship and leads to better conversations, network building, and opportunities down the road for everyone involved.

2. **Using RFPs to find high-quality consultants.** Most of our business, like that of any consultant worth his or

her cost, comes from referrals. Generally speaking—though not always—the consultants who have time to respond to multiple RFPs either aren't getting enough repeat or referral business or they need to charge high fees to compensate for all the staff time spent submitting proposals. If this is the case, these probably aren't the best consultants to choose among. There are, of course, exceptions. All consultants—I include myself—have hit highs when business is flowing and lows when business is scarce, often due to changing external environments or lack of their own marketing and business development.

What's better: I have successfully responded to RFPs that resulted in large, multi-year engagements for which we were able to add tremendous value. But in those cases, I had built relationships with the clients over many years and had opportunities for extensive discussions with them about their needs and objectives—neither of which are supported through the typical RFP process. Both the client and I knew this would be a high-quality engagement for both of us, because we already had a relationship. That's why I'd take three strong referrals over three unknown proposals any day. Referrals are built on positive relationships. RFPs are built on assumptions and guesswork.

3. **Using RFPs to demonstrate transparency.**
   Foundations are under pressure to be transparent, and they should be—they are stewards of the public trust. They often view sending an RFP to multiple consultants as one way to demonstrate transparency, because they aren't picking the specific consultant (often called "sole sourcing") "behind closed doors." But there is very little that's transparent in the RFP process. Foundations don't publicize which consultants they choose to invite or what criteria they use to identify them. Nor do they

publicize how they make their final determination, which is always "behind closed doors" anyway. The process is least transparent to the consultants themselves, who typically have little opportunity to meet with the ultimate decision makers and therefore have no way of fully understanding the foundation's needs or objectives regarding a specific project. They often aren't told why they were chosen to submit a proposal and are rarely told whom they are competing against or even how many people they are competing against. While most RFPs outline a specific scope of services and time line, the consultant has no idea how or why this was determined, or if it even makes sense.

What's better: Instead of creating an RFP process, the foundation could invest less of its own staff time and yield a better result by seeking referrals for consultants and then inviting the best of those consultants in for meaningful conversations with decision makers, being open about who else the foundation is talking to, what plans and questions it is considering, and how it ultimately will make its decision.

4. **Requiring RFPs to hire consultants.** An evaluation director of a private foundation told me that it's their policy to use RFPs when hiring any evaluator, and they generally ask at least three evaluators to submit proposals. This makes little sense and is frankly a waste of time and resources. If a foundation knows of a terrific consultant or evaluator with whom they have worked before, who has demonstrated high-quality results, is qualified to do the work, and whom they want to hire, why wouldn't the foundation just hire that consultant again and save everyone time and money? It may be that foundations consider obtaining multiple proposals to be a measure of financial stewardship, but is it really good stewardship to continually invest in an RFP process if you've already secured good value?

Trading efficiency for transparency can waste precious philanthropic resources that could be better allocated to advance the foundation's mission. It also smacks of micromanagement. If you hire talented staff, you should trust them to choose talented consultants.

What's better: Instead of mandating policy that requires an RFP process every time, trust yourself and your staff to know when there's a better and more efficient way to hire a consultant. The point is not that it's a bad idea to issue a request for proposals—it's just a bad idea to limit yourself and waste your resources with an unnecessary requirement. When issuing an RFP is the best way to get what you need, go for it. Otherwise, use the tips below to find a high-quality consultant—and save your time and resources for more urgent needs.

Five better ways to find and retain quality consulting help

Based on my experience and that of other consultants and organizations I know, there are other—and better—ways to find a great consultant to help you with your project. **Before you send out another RFP, consider these alternatives:**

1. **Continuously source and build relationships with consultants.** Don't wait until you desperately need a consultant to start looking for one. Ask peer foundations to share their experiences with you. Better yet, create a shared list of consultants who have delivered pleasing results. Even if you're just beginning to think about a project, ask a consultant or two to help you brainstorm ideas in the early stages in exchange for lunch.

2. **Ask colleagues, including consultants, for referrals.** Word of mouth truly is the best source. Send an email to colleagues in your foundation and at other foundations, briefly describing what you're looking for and asking for

suggestions. Listservs or directories provided by funder networks, affinity groups, and regional associations can also provide valuable contacts and referrals.

3. **Turn to the National Network of Consultants to Grantmakers (NNCG).** NNCG's mission is to increase the quality, effectiveness, and capacity of grantmakers by mobilizing and strengthening the work of knowledgeable, ethical, and experienced consultants. It hosts a free online directory that offers a complete list of vetted consultants across the country and in multiple disciplines.

4. **Issue a "Request for Qualifications" instead of a Request for Proposals.** It is much less time consuming for you to prepare an RFQ and review all the responses, and for the consultant to submit a two-page list of qualifications. You will likely identify terrific consultants who aren't the right fit for this particular project but who might be good for future needs. Keep their information as part of your consultant sourcing efforts (see #1 above).

5. **Be open and honest with prospective consultants about what you are doing,** what you are looking for, and the stage you are in. If you want some free advice, tell them that, limit their time, and buy them breakfast or lunch. If you need more of their time, pay them for a half or full day to come in and brainstorm and vet ideas, with no expectations of any further work.

If you strongly prefer to use an RFP process (or if you are trapped under your foundation's RFP policy), here are five suggestions to make it as successful as possible:

1. Limit the number of consultants invited to submit proposals. A director of evaluation at a community foundation near San Francisco once invited me to

respond to an RFP. I asked him how many other evaluators he reached out to. "I invited 50 evaluators to submit proposals, and I prequalified all of them by reviewing information about them on their websites and evaluators' directories," he proudly stated. This was for a relatively small project. I politely declined. He later told me that he was so overwhelmed in reviewing all the proposals that he had to completely reprioritize his workload.

2. As you create your RFP, encourage meaningful opportunities for discussion with prospective consultants so that they can help you identify your objectives, measures of success, and the value to your organization. This will result in higher-quality proposals, mutual agreement of goals, and superior results. Instead of sending an email that says, "You are invited to submit a proposal by this deadline; see attached," pick up the phone and discuss the project with your short list of consultants.

3. Provide opportunities for prospective consultants to talk with decision makers. A consultant must understand the needs and objectives of the people whose budgets are funding the project, to ensure that the proposal meets those needs.

4. Don't pretend to know everything about the project. Sometimes you might not be in the best position to determine the specific scope of work, but you can allow the consultant you retain to help do that. Focus the RFP on your needs, your goals and objectives for the project, and critical deadlines. Instead of specifying that you need ten focus groups and a survey, let the consultant use his or her knowledge and experience to help you determine the best approach to meet your stated goals.

5. Tell the consultants why you have invited them to apply, and let them know the others who are competing for this work. I once convinced a group of health funders to tell me whom I would be competing against if I responded to an RFP, and I was given the names of large, statewide nonprofit research and advocacy organizations, as well as several universities. I quickly concluded that either they threw me into the mix as an outlier to see what I came up with, or they had no idea what type of help they needed. Either way, I realized, responding to their RFP would be a waste of my time and theirs.

I'm not saying that RFPs never generate talented, effective consultants. I am sure many readers of this article have an example of terrific consulting expertise they obtained through an RFP process. However, I suggest that instead of turning to an RFP as the default, foundations might be better served by checking their assumptions about the value of this process, considering the actual human and financial resources involved in executing it, and brainstorming other ways of engaging consultants that involve honesty, trust, and relationship building.

●　　●　　●

HOW TO EFFECTIVELY HIRE A CONSULTANT: FIVE TIPS FOR A WIN-WIN RELATIONSHIP

Nonprofit and foundation leaders are held accountable to their stakeholders to make sure they're using their budgets to garner the best results. A strong relationship with quality consultants can help limited budgets go a long way, so it's imperative that you find a consultant who can become a valuable member of your team. Here are few guidelines to help you succeed when working with consultants.

1. **Understand all your goals.** First, take the time to fully understand the problems you want to resolve. Be clear about what you expect the consultant to accomplish and identify all the key stakeholders who may need to be engaged in the project. Engage your consultant in helping you think through your objectives. It's also essential to identify any barriers the project's success, and to be clear about your time frame and budget.

2. **Identify the right consultant.** Once your goals are clearly outlined, find a consultant with the right skills and experience. Would you prefer to work with a sole proprietor or a large consulting firm? What capacity do they need to scale up a large project? Do you need a consultant who knows your local community, or would it help to get an outside perspective? Do they need specific content expertise (e.g., workforce development) or process expertise (e.g., conducting focus groups)? Then be sure to check references and conduct due diligence before finalizing an agreement. The Consultant Directory compiled by the National Network of Consultants to Grantmakers can help you identify quality consultants.

3. **Establish a clear relationship.** When you initiate a project with a new consultant, you're laying the foundation for a relationship that could prove highly beneficial for many years to come. Explain your needs clearly and answer any questions the consultant may have. Be sure to agree upon the scope of work and on how you'll work together. Finally, provide your consultant with all the necessary introductions, along with background information and, if needed, infrastructure support.

4. **Manage for success.** Even with the best consultant on your team, you won't be able to delegate everything, so be sure to build in enough time to manage your project.

You may want to check in with your consultant on a regular basis to air any concerns, troubleshoot potential problems, or discuss findings. Remember that if you add deliverables to the contract, the fee and time line may also need to be extended.

5. **Conclude and debrief the engagement.** It's important to officially conclude your engagement when it's complete. Meet with your consultant to provide feedback and discuss how you intend to put the findings to work in your organization. Have an honest conversation about the consulting relationship and discuss ways you might work more effectively together in the future. We all learn from experience, and this is where you both have the greatest opportunity to voice what you learned.

5 STEPS TO EFFECTIVELY HIRING A CONSULTANT

Conclude
and debrief
the engagement

Manage
for success

Establish a
clear relationship

Identify
the right
consultant

Understand
your goals

When you enter your relationship with a consultant with a shared, clear understanding of your goals, roles, and expectations, you are on your way to a successful endeavor.

● ● ●

DON'T NEED A CONSULTANT? FIVE GOOD REASONS YOU MIGHT BE WRONG

Foundation and nonprofit staff are spread thin enough. And sometimes expecting hardworking staff to strategize and carry through an entirely new project, on top of handling their ongoing responsibilities, is asking too much.

Consultants can take some of the burden off of staff while providing perspective and expertise. They may also increase your organization's credibility. Here are five reasons most foundations and nonprofits enlist outside consultants.

1. **Time.** Staff temporarily busy, or not enough staff? A consultant can fill in for a staff member on leave or serve as a "staff extender" to an existing team. For example, one of my family foundation clients was growing quickly. The CEO planned to hire more program officers—after she developed new grantmaking programs. Meanwhile she retained me to review proposals, conduct site visits, and research new grantmaking strategies. She added staff capacity without making any long-term commitments.

2. **Expertise.** Rarely can we have all the skills we need on staff at any given time. Consultants can fill in the gaps with expert knowledge or with specialized skills in research, evaluation, facilitation, strategic planning, marketing, and more. You can hire a consultant with

preexisting knowledge, or one without content expertise who brings a fresh perspective.

3. **Objectivity.** The best solution is not always the most obvious one. For example, if you want to get at the underlying reasons teens don't succeed in school, an outside consultant can provide much-needed objectivity. A consultant can be a "neutral voice," conducting objective research, assessing opportunities, and developing new solutions.

4. **Openness.** Nonprofits often feel they can't disclose their real challenges—they're worried that they'll lose your funding. An outside consultant, however, can inspire a sense of confidentiality, then explain the issues and concerns to you without sharing exactly who raised them. Nonprofits, grantees, and stakeholders often feel more comfortable telling a consultant what's really happening and what's really needed.

5. **Credibility.** A consultant can increase a project's credibility in the eyes of the target audience. For example, an organization seeking to replicate a program across multiple states might hire a nationally known evaluation firm to inspire confidence among national funders. For a grassroots effort, you might hire a community-based consulting firm with experience in your target region.

No matter what your goal, hiring a consultant may be the right next step.

● ● ●

DO YOU TRUST YOUR CONSULTANT?

The CEO of a prestigious family foundation once told me that one of the main reasons she retained me as a consultant was that when I walked in the door, all her staff—from the receptionist to the tech guys to the program staff—were happy to see me. I easily fit in to her team and their culture, she explained.

Another client frequently came to my house for daylong brainstorming and planning sessions. I lived in a tranquil, wooded setting. He felt relaxed, I'd make lunch, and by the end of the day my living room was filled with easel paper jam-packed with ideas, clarity, and next steps.

When I worked at Stanford University evaluating youth violence-prevention programs, a new colleague observed me at a conference talking with all the community organizations we were evaluating. Shocked, he said, "I can't believe everyone gave you hugs! Most people don't hug their evaluator."

All of these stories remind me that the single most important factor of a successful consultant-foundation relationship is trust. Yes, your consultant needs to be qualified to help you, bringing the experience and skills to the table that will further your efforts and add value. But that value is greatly lessened, or even damaged, if trust is not present.

Trust can be defined as simply maintaining confidentiality or shared respect, but it really goes much deeper. Most of the time, the work that needs to be done in a consulting engagement requires some sort of change, whether it's simply getting used to a new face on the team or making a small tweak in an existing process to creating a wholesale shift in strategy or launching something completely new and different. No matter what kind of change is involved, our human nature demands that we trust those suggesting or working through change with us. If we don't feel that trust, we will find ways to resist.

As a consultant, how do you establish trust?

- **Be yourself.** Authenticity is far more important than having an MBA from Harvard, a long list of prestigious clients, or any other flag consultants want to wave in front of their clients. You must let people see who you are before they can form a trusting relationship with you.

- **Turn down business that is not congruent with your values, expertise, and skills.** We all need to pay the mortgage, but not at the expense of learning on the foundation's dime or, worse, working with someone we don't like or don't believe in. You can't establish trust when you aren't qualified for the job or it causes you undue stress.

- **Spend time intentionally building the relationship.** When I am talking to a potential client, I will gladly get on a plane at my own expense to meet with them. That is how important the relationship is to me and to the success of the engagement. My clients need to decide if I am the right fit for them, and I need to know that they are the right fit for me.

DETERMINING WHEN TO TRUST YOUR CONSULTANT

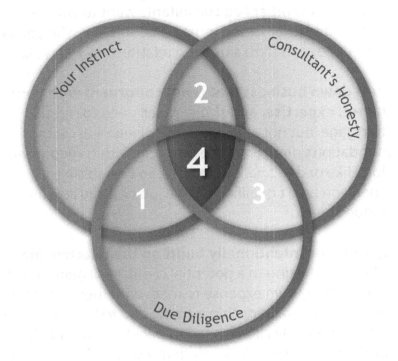

1. POSSIBLE "YES-MAN"
2. NO TRACK RECORD
3. HIGH POTENTIAL TO FAIL
4. **TRUSTWORTHY FUNDER-CONSULTANT RELATIONSHIP**

As a funder, how do you know if you can trust your consultant?

- **Trust your instinct.** A consultant can be good on paper, with all the right degrees, experience, and board affiliations. But suspend all of that and for a moment

152

focus on what your gut tells you. The consultant might be the right fit for someone else, but not for you.

- **Don't confuse trust with someone who tells you what you want to hear.** A consultant who simply reaffirms what you want to do so as not to rock the boat may not actually be trustworthy and may not truly respect you. A good consultant brings wisdom and perspective and should be willing to push back, challenge your assumptions, and ask, "Why?" It shouldn't be painful, but occasional discomfort can be a good sign of a healthy consultant-client relationship.

- **Do your due diligence.** Call the consultant's past clients and ask questions to determine whether he or she is trustworthy. These questions might include: Did you feel you could share sensitive information with this consultant? Did he keep confidential matters confidential? Did she represent you and your foundation well in external meetings? Did you enjoy working with her? What was your staff's experience working with him?

Foundations use consultants for a number of reasons—and those engagements can be highly satisfactory when mutual trust exists. Parties on both sides of the equation owe it to one another—and to themselves—to ensure that trust is a cornerstone of any consulting relationship.

CONSULTANTS CAN TAKE SOME OF THE BURDEN OFF STAFF WHILE PROVIDING A NEW PERSPECTIVE AND EXPERTISE.

• • •

Afterword

I hope you've enjoyed reading this book, and that you'll share it with your friends and colleagues in the field. If there's one thing I've learned during my years as a consultant to philanthropy, it's that you can never stop learning about philanthropy. I continue to be humbled and amazed by all the brilliant minds and phenomenal ideas that have influenced my practice, and I am honored to share what I know whenever I can.

Along those lines, if you have an interest in learning more about philanthropy and funding, I encourage you to visit my website at www.putnam-consulting.com and to explore the host of resources there. My goal is to make it easy to grab a few pearls of wisdom quickly and incorporate them into your philanthropic practice immediately. **I invite you to:**

- **Read a blog post.** The Philanthropy 411 blog contains thought-provoking ideas and insights from my clients and other philanthropy experts as well as from me. Have each new post delivered directly to your email inbox via RSS, and share what you read via your own social media networks.
- **Listen to a podcast.** Stream an informative, concise podcast and hear great tips for improving your grantmaking practice. Learn how to increase impact, think creatively about funding, build better relationships with key stakeholders, and much more.
- **Study a case study.** Want to see how different foundations tackled the same problems you may be facing? Peruse a Putnam case study to see exactly what your peers and colleagues did when faced with challenges of grantmaking, information sharing, strategy development, and other aspects of foundation operations.
- **Read and share an article.** We have dozens of articles that provide guidance on best practice program design, smart asset allocation, evaluation, communications, and getting the most out of your consulting partners.
- **Subscribe to the *Confident Giving*® newsletter.**

That's just a quick sample of what's available on the Putnam Consulting Group website. I know you will find it to be of great value, and I invite you to explore it at putnam-consulting.com. And, I would love to hear your thoughts, experiences, and suggestions for topics for the *Confident Giving*® newsletter and other resources, to make them even more useful and relevant to your work. Contact me any time at kris@putnam-consulting.com.

I look forward to helping you give confidently for dramatic return on the issues and communities you care about!

— **Kris Putnam-Walkerly, MSW**

About the Author

For more than 16 years, top global philanthropies have requested Kris Putnam-Walkerly's help to transform their giving and catapult their impact, including designing strategies that achieve results, understanding their impact, and allocating funds. Her clients include the Robert Wood Johnson, David and Lucile Packard, Winthrop Rockefeller, Annie E. Casey, Charles and Helen Schwab, and Kate B. Reynolds Charitable Trust, among others.

Kris is a thought leader in transformative philanthropy and was recently named one of America's Top 25 Philanthropy Speakers. She is a frequent contributor in the publications of leading philanthropy associations, including the National Center for Family Philanthropy, Southeastern Council on Foundations, and Exponent Philanthropy.

She provides expert commentary about philanthropy in the *Wall Street Journal*, *Washington Post*, *Seattle Times*, *Washington Examiner*, Entepreneur.com, BusinessWeek.com, and others. Kris was selected to co-edit *The Foundation Review*'s themed journal on philanthropy consulting and the Grants Managers Network's journal on streamlining philanthropy.

Kris chairs the board of the National Network of Consultants to Grantmakers and serves on the board of the Community Foundation of Lorain County and the Advisory Committee of the Foundation Center in Cleveland. Kris and her firm have received accolades, including a "Top 10 Women Business Owners" award in 2008 from the National Association of Women Business Owners – Cleveland and a "Ten Under 10" award in 2008 from the Council of Smaller Enterprises.

Prior to forming Putnam Consulting Group, she was a grantmaker at the David and Lucile Packard Foundation and an evaluator at the highly esteemed Stanford University School of Medicine. Kris holds a master's degree in social work from San Francisco State University and a bachelor's degree from Indiana University. She and her husband have five children, and reside near Cleveland, Ohio.